Memory, Recall, the Brain & Learning

IMPROVE STUDENT LEARNING OUTCOMES

By Engaging Learners in Visual and Nonlinguistic
Strategies, Activities, and Organizers

By

Dr. Robert K. Greenleaf

Doris Wells-Papanek

Greenleaf & Papanek **Publications**

Memory, Recall, the Brain & Learning

IMPROVE STUDENT LEARNING OUTCOMES
By Engaging Learners in Visual and Nonlinguistic
Strategies, Activities, and Organizers

Former Title: (First Printing, 2005) *Knowledge Representation and the Brain*
The Nonlinguistic and Visual Attributes of Memory and Recall

Greenleaf & Papanek **Publications**

Contact
Information

Dr. Robert K. Greenleaf
P.O. Box 186
Newfield, Maine 04056
207.793.8675 tel.
207.604.0089 cell

bob@greenleaflearning.com
www.greenleaflearning.com

Doris Wells-Papanek
1521 Heritage Court
Lake Forest, Illinois 60045
847.615.9957 tel.
847.615.9958 fax

doris@tailoredlearningtools.com
www.tailoredlearningtools.com

ISBN: 0-9767860-1-X

Dedication

To the capable,
struggling learners whose minds are fertile,
and more fully engaged when
visual realities are part of their learning.

To the partnership of people and ideas.

Memory, Recall, the Brain & Learning

IMPROVE STUDENT LEARNING OUTCOMES
By Engaging Learners in Visual and Nonlinguistic Strategies, Activities, and Organizers

Table of Contents

SECTION ONE   *Overview*

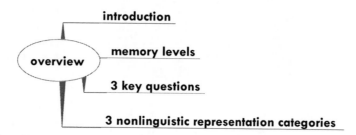

Brain research, though historically focused on abnormalities and pharmaceuticals, has evidenced unprecedented levels of attention in education and learning endeavors. We have come to understand that "learning" is not merely an exercise in storing information for artificially engineered tests. Our interest and intent have evolved to encompass the notions of recall, long-term memory, and applications - not to mention life-long learning habits.

Our goal in teaching and learning must be to create environments and conditions in which learners are more likely to make greater attempts at processing sufficiently for understanding and application, resulting in increased long-term memory. This book seeks to explore in detail a vital aspect of learning and the brain that supports the acquisition of sustained understanding.

The following illustration (Fig. 1) may be useful as a graphic to consider in thinking about this process. We use the metaphor of a "barn" as a storage area for long-term memory. As information enters the body/brain through the senses, it is instantly regarded across many levels (a threat, of interest, of no consequence, etc.). As a result, the vast majority of stimuli that enter the brain are discarded momentarily - much without conscious awareness. The challenge is to construct learning opportunities that cause sufficient processing in short-term memory (desktop) such that it spawns activity across synapses resulting in long-term memory or to link new information and ideas with those already in the "barn." When we draw on information already deemed worthy of being in the barn and process new information in context with it, the likelihood that the new information will remain in long-term memory is increased.

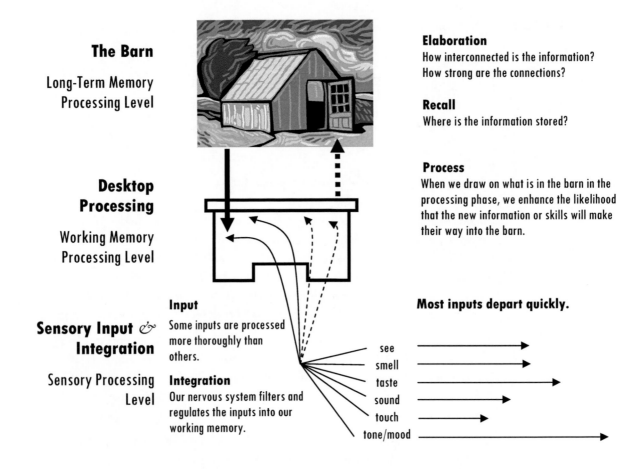

The Barn

Long-Term Memory
Processing Level

Elaboration
How interconnected is the information?
How strong are the connections?

Recall
Where is the information stored?

Process
When we draw on what is in the barn in the processing phase, we enhance the likelihood that the new information or skills will make their way into the barn.

Desktop Processing

Working Memory
Processing Level

Sensory Input & **Integration**

Sensory Processing Level

Input
Some inputs are processed more thoroughly than others.

Integration
Our nervous system filters and regulates the inputs into our working memory.

Most inputs depart quickly.

see
smell
taste
sound
touch
tone/mood

Figure 1: Memory is Divided into a Multiple Level Process

Sensory Input — Basic levels of processing in the brain are commonly discussed in three levels. The most basic level (bottom) is sensory. At this level, inputs enter the brain via the senses. This book seeks to explore in detail a vital aspect of learning and the brain that supports the acquisition of sustained understanding. Realizing that the brain processes these in quick fashion, most inputs and understandings are immediately discarded in favor of items of higher interest or that are personal (the fact that a red car has passed by is hardly as important as the familiar person walking in our direction). While we "see/hear" a great deal, most does not appear important to us, thus we readily dismiss it.

Working Memory   The middle level is our working memory or "desktop," which refers to brain activity that is processed in a longer or more involved manner. Connections to meaning, patterns or a link to other previously noticed items are sought. This in no way insures adequate learning, but does constitute additional thought, interest, or attention to the input, for organization, categorization, understanding, or some other purposeful activity. Working memory activity is the general path to long-term memory.

Long-Term Memory   The highest level refers to long-term memory. Though some things may achieve long-term status more quickly through an emotional episode or novelty, the vast amount of inputs require more substantive processing prior to semi- or permanent memory conditions. When the brain "pulls" prior experience, knowledge or ideas from what is already residing in the metaphoric "barn" (long-term memory) and considers the new information in relation to it, the chances of the new input being incorporated into memory for a longer duration increases dramatically.

In the end, it all comes down to sustaining capacities. Our work is to generate opportunities that learners can... and will take advantage of - to engage.

In the book "Brain Based Teaching: Making Connections for Long-Term Memory and Recall," by Greenleaf, three big questions were framed that drive the learning agenda through the brain sciences and long-term memory. If the context of the learning situation embraces these questions as the overarching dynamics that create a circumstance that supports, even prompts, the very activity required in the brain for processing and ultimate memory to be formed - then we have achieved our purpose - but not short of retrieval. Can the learner access pertinent information at appropriate future times? These questions serve to keep us focused on the desired outcomes that we require from the process of teaching.

Question #1   How can I "frame" (design) the learning circumstance or activity so that it *INVITES ALL* learners to get involved, to participate?

How do we engineer opportunities that "pull" learners into the activity? Are there ways to design tasks that are compelling enough to tap into learner interest, intrigue, and purpose, such that choices are made to participate rather than to place attention in other, less constructive endeavors?

Question #2   How can I design the learning experience such that it will *CAUSE* learners to process, to do the work required for sustained learning to take place?

External activity cannot be mistaken for internal processing. All the interactive strategies and options to manipulate objects - well intended as they are - must result in the brain doing the necessary processing to stimulate, create, and integrate new connections. She or he who works, learns.

Question #3   How do I engineer tasks that create opportunities for multiple *PATHWAYS* to be formed (connections made) for integrated learning, application and recall?

When students become readers, even with minimal skills, the "diet" of activities shifts in large part from direct instruction with visual guides, to a heavy dose of linguistics (reading, writing, discussion, etc.). While this diet nourishes some brain systems/pathways, it is inadequate to stimulate and integrate in a comprehensive manner. To their credit, some learners are exceptionally skilled at reading or interacting with new information one time - and memory seems to be secured. The question remains, can learners integrate and transfer new learnings to other and varied circumstances? If we store information only to regurgitate it from the same module in the brain time and time again, we have limited accomplishment - as we fall prey to required cues that tap into recall only via that one venue. The process of creating multiple links, neuronal connections across many lobes and modules, provides a rich opportunity for increased recall, transfer, insight and applications reaching beyond the confines of subject matter in a content area.

SECTION TWO *Nonlinguistic Representation (NLRs) Strategies*

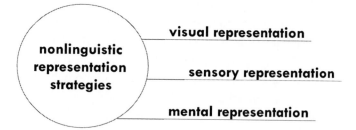

The Focus of the Book — Left on our own, we all create and access imagery in our minds. However, when teachers prompt the use of nonlinguistics in tandem with verbal modes, the effects on learning and achievement are powerful. Explicit instruction and requests for students to use a variety of visually engaging venues increases brain activity (Gerlic & Jausovec). When the learner interacts with complimentary, but different modes of the same information, the level of understanding, retention and recall increase. This process is called elaboration - well documented in the memory process.

Nonlinguistic representations can take many forms. They can be generated by teacher or learner in external fashion (graphic organizers, drawings, pictures, movement) or from within the learner (prior experience and knowledge, imagery, imagination, sensory reflections). Exposing learners to representations that are provided by the publisher or the teacher helps to create bi-modal packets. When students either create their own representations in a medium or generate visuals in their minds, similar memory benefits occur.

For the purposes of this book, we have devised three main categories of nonlinguistic representations for you to consider in the classroom. Clearly, researchers vary in their vocabulary and organization of the terms and approaches, which can be confusing. Depending on the researcher or author, nonlinguistics could be viewed as visual representations, physical models, drawings, mental imagery, sensory venues, or bodily kinesthetic activity. For sure, room for exploration is multifaceted and vast. Some will find more comfort if representations concretely align with cognitive tasks.

The three categories we will use to organize the varied options are Visual Representations, Sensory Representations, and Mental Representations. Each category is explained in the following text, with accompanying descriptions. Later in the book, examples of discrete activities are outlined for each one.

Category 1 *Visual Representation*

This category of nonlinguistic representations consists of two-dimensional constructs that can be formed simply with pencil and paper (or other mediums as desired). These can be drawings, webs, frameworks that organize ideas and information, graphs, symbolic pictures, mind maps, etc. Nonlinguistic representations serve to represent relationships between two or more items, illustrate meaning, or establish priorities of importance. The process is designed to mirror the natural way the mind creates and integrates networks for memory structures.

In essence, we are generating physical representations that are analogous to the brain's internal processing of verbal-visual bimodal packets. These form "micro" packets that are members of larger information sets that lump together into categories of information.

In a review of nonlinguistic representations, Marzano et. al. (2001) outlined the following types of patterns that might be captured.

- **Descriptive Patterns** — representing facts or multiple related items.

- **Time-Sequence patterns** — organizing events in chronological order.

- **Cause/Effect or Process Patterns** — sequencing steps or relationships between things.

- **Episode Patterns** — organizing information regarding a specific event.

- **Generalization/Principle Patterns** — organize information into main ideas and supporting details.

- **Concept Patterns** — organized around a word, phrase or idea that represents a big idea or overarching concept. Categories and sub-categories are formed in context to the big idea.

The strategies and activities later in this book offer a variety of applications across many of these areas. In addition, a number of organizers are provided for a variety of applications.

Category 2   *Sensory Representation*

Stimulus from the outside world enters our bodies through the senses. This flow is a two-way enterprise. We can touch things and we can be touched. We can see things that are outside of us and we can generate images internally. We can move toward something and some things can move toward us. Our senses are essential links to the world we are trying to make sense of - to comprehend and even master.

As we integrate our sensory inputs with existing internal information, we explore new patterns, ideas, and notions in an endless effort to understand. Using our sensory mode provides yet another nonlinguistic venue. From movement, to touch, to body in space proximity, our spatial senses create sensory understandings and, when viable, triangulate retrieval cues for recall.

Movement   We've learned much about manipulatives - the act of physically moving objects to assist the process of understanding sequence, procedure or even simply to "feel" the experience in addition to thinking it. We practice skills (kicking a ball, writing letters) repetitiously, in attempts to improve and master capacity. Moving can be a whole body (gross motor) relocation or a more subtle (fine motor) partial body action. We can emulate physical constructs of mental images and prior experiences (mirroring a plant growing, unfurling into the sunlight by moving from a crouched, low position to a standing, arms extended position). We can move components of a unit around to sense how they interact and work together. We can organize objects into a chronological or sequential order, we can reposition ourselves to alter perspective.

In the end, much of the brain's real estate is involved with the myriad of options available through our physical learning system. As we accommodate this system, we create multiple pathways for experiences and understandings to form.

Body in Space   This option is often underutilized. It need not require continual movement, but more importantly, the location or disposition of our "being" in a context. If we are asked to physically write down a response to a query prior to a class discussion, we have mentally "positioned" our self. We've made a commitment. This triggers a different series of brain activity than passive thought. Similarly, if we are asked to commit by moving our entire body to a location (field trip) we experience things in a more concrete manner than abstract. Taking this a step further, when a learner physically moves to a designated place in the class (under a banner, to a group, or along a continuum on the wall) that serves as a statement (I believe this or I am choosing the topic or approach this group is using). This process enables the student to anchor content of an experience in a context, generating multiple memory structures and more probable opportunities for retrieval.

Touch   Saul Schanberg says that touch is "ten times stronger than verbal or emotional contact, and it affects damn near everything we do. No other sense can arouse you like touch." Barbara Given quoted in her book on natural learning systems, that "… when liked and groomed by their mothers, rat pups produced growth hormones, but when pups were removed from mother's care, their production of growth hormones dropped."

We are all aware that a caring hug or positive touch on our arm prompts a wealth of sensation and reaction - both physical and emotional. Touch adds a dimension to our processing that cannot be replicated in other ways. The physical act of interacting with something (swinging a hammer, dancing to music, moving objects to order them in a sequence, reaching out and touching something to feel it's outer layer) or having something interact with you (receiving a pat on the back, being in a place when a significant event happens [9-11], having sunlight heat your face or feeling a waterfall pour over you) establishes a context in which learning can be secured, referenced and transferred to other applications.

Category 3 *Mental Representation*

Our minds generate internal imagery in an ongoing manner. It's endless. If we pay attention, we notice that each internal image we create is accompanied by a feeling or emotion. Sometimes it is the sense of wonder or novelty that we feel. Other times, the cascade of feelings are strong and distinctly attached to the event, person or topic we are exploring in our mind. Consciously, deliberately tapping into this natural process in the brain serves to "piggy-back" on existing energies the mind is already using. There is much literature regarding the role of emotion in long-term memory formation. It is a powerful "cement" as well as retrieval cue.

Explicit instruction to make an effort to consider or link internal imagery has been shown to impact performance outcomes. Our past experiences and knowledge come to bear on our interpretations in the present; in our attempts to make sense of new ideas, information and understandings.

Forming images in our minds is something seldom requested of learners. Yet, if we take the time to ask students to reference images they have formed or to create new ones and take note of them - these can serve as "vehicles" that "carry" the new information or learning. At times, a student may have little experience or prior exposure to a subject and the teacher will need to provide some external imagery (photos, pictures, drawings, paintings, etc.). However, as the studies suggest, it is more powerful to form one's own, or to do both - to use provided representations as well as to reference internal ones.

Example   In concert with a unit of study try this: "Imagine you are living during this time and you are the first person to stumble upon the Grand Canyon," or "Your vessel has landed on the planet of Saturn. As you look out into space, what do you see? How do the rings appear from where you are standing?" or "Picture yourself on top of a ten story building, dropping two objects - a baseball and a nerf ball. What do you see them doing in comparison to one another?" or "If we did not have the wheel, how would traveling from one place to another be different?" or "Pause, close your eyes. Can you see the worm traveling through the earth's soil? Go deeper into the ground. Deeper. What do you eventually run into? And then what?"

Junior High School students demonstrated the impact of mental imagery in a reported by Zemke (1981). Students were divided into three groups. One group practiced the basketball skill of foul shooting by practicing daily. The control group did not practice at all. The third group, the mental imagery group, was instructed to form the sequence of mental pictures corresponding with standing at the foul line, bouncing the ball as they normally would, looking up at the hoop, going through their motion, releasing the ball and watching it sail through the hoop in a "swish" every time. They practiced this imagery for the same amount of time the first group physically practiced actual foul shooting. After two weeks, the control group did not improve in ability to make baskets from the foul line. The other two groups improved equivalently. The mental imagery produced the same outcome as the actual physical activity. The mind is a powerful tool!

Comprehensive Research and Support is the Foundation for the Work Put Forward in this Book

Beneath the focal purpose of this book is a breadth of support from research and experience. The studies and activities presented can certainly stand on their own merit(s). However, it is our intent to actively merge brain science research and educational best practice. To that end, we have selected two profound works as the foundation for the strategies we have developed. From the neuroscience side of the equation, we embrace the model put forward by Dr. Barbara Given in her work on the natural learning systems of the brain. From the educational side, we build on the meta-analyses done by Marzano, Pickering, and Pollock in 2001, on the nine most effective educational strategies leading to student achievement.

SECTION THREE *Barbara Given ~ 5 Natural Learning Systems*

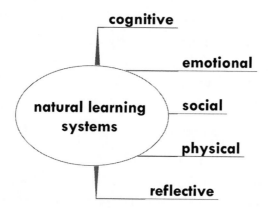

Recently, Dr. Barbara Given compiled an impressive array of timely, pertinent and valid research. From this, she developed a viable, practical model for considering the brain's natural processing functions as they relate to the teaching/learning intersection. These five natural systems are cognitive, emotional, social, physical, and reflective. (ASCD 2002)

Comprehensive systems for receiving, processing and recalling information are thoroughly integrated throughout brain areas. Though we see evidence of localized activity through fMRI and PET scan studies, these "areas of activity" do not represent ALL activity - they represent where the initial or most of the activity takes place. Still, it is important to understand that within moments other areas are involved in major, minor or peripheral ways. Bottom line: the brain is so integrated that localization of regional activity is useful for research purposes, but less directly applicable for instructional practice.

If we understand this model, then we are compelled to offer opportunities to learners that serve to prompt each learning system over the course of a unit of study or series of lessons. By doing so, we differentiate instructional approaches, vary strategies, prompt processing in working memory and build multiple pathways for retention, recall, transfer, and application of learnings... in short, for understanding.

Cognitive System

- Actions that we perform based on an explicit intention.

- Requires integrated prior knowledge and skills.

- Cognition enables us to construct or problem-solve output using pattern, concept or theme.

- Enables us to read, write, and calculate.

- Enables us to interpret, store, and retrieve information.

- Can be overrun by stress response system and other perceived priorities.

The Cognitive Learning System pertains to reading, writing, calculation and other aspects of academic skill development. Most education and assessment tends to focus on the outputs of this system. Below are some quotes to help orient the reader to the work of Barbara Given on this natural learning system.

Historically, most teachers typically "taught discrete bits of information to be memorized, rather than information patterns, concepts, and themes. When not making connections between new information and what students already know or the context in which it is found, teaching for memorization goes against how the cognitive learning system actually functions." (p. 80)

"Whenever the emotional or social systems are in turmoil, the cognitive system must spend its energy on them before it can focus on the higher order thinking required for knowledge and skill acquisition. It operates best when other systems are not competing with it for attention." (p.81)

"The cognitive system thrives on mental challenge and problem solving. This system's need to know states a genetic truth in simple terms. Humans are designed to learn. Learning is as natural as breathing, and it cannot be stopped short of brain damage." (p. 82) For example:

- Write new lyrics to "Twinkle-Twinkle Little Star"

- Build a concept with rods and explain how it conveys the idea(s)

- Illustrate major points on a poster

- Recite a "rap" rhythm that includes major points

Individual Perceptions

"What a person perceives is not a direct or accurate representation of reality, but an elaboration based on unconscious inferences due to expectations and past perceptions." (Guenther, 1998)

Two students may react quite differently to a poster showing various brain lobes and an announcement that the next thematic science unit will focus on the nervous system.

- A student with low reading skills and limited success in science may perceive only the portions of the poster that accentuate his weaknesses. He immediately believes that his skills are inadequate to the task, fails to see any positive aspects of the project, and responds with worry.

- Another student, whose background is richly endowed, may perceive abundant detail and look forward to the experience as an exciting new learning opportunity. (p. 63-64)

Reading and Auditory Processing (p.67)

Specific instruction in phonemic awareness is critical as early as possible to help children establish discrete networks before a single collective neural network becomes firmly entrenched and similar sounds are perceived as one. Preschool alphabet books can serve as prompts in helping children make those discriminations. "I see something that begins with the sound /b/. Can you guess what it is?" Without accuracy in fine discriminations, oral language difficulties soon become apparent and reading difficulties soon follow.

Emotional System

- With personal meaning comes relevance and a passion for learning.

- Emotions can empower and energize (or depress and stifle) all other learning systems.

- Class climate and emotional safety are closely linked to a student's success.

- Zone of proximal development: by minimizing anxiety we can help regulate internal stress responses to activities.

- Emotion is a powerful vehicle to enhance memory, manage our demeanor, and increase creativity.

Unless a classroom climate that is conducive to a sense of emotional safety and personal relevancy for students is established, children will not learn effectively, and may reject our efforts regarding their education altogether. This system is personal, self-absorbed and internally driven.

The following three quotes help orient the reader to the work of Barbara Given on this natural learning system.

"...without acceptance and emotional support energy needed for developing new skills may be spent seeking positive affirmations and guarding against abuse, ridicule, sarcasm, embarrassment, isolation, loneliness and rejection." (p. 15) [p.24 = further explanations]

"Teachers who nourish the emotional system serve as mentors for students by demonstrating sincere enthusiasm for their subject; by helping students discover a passion for learning; by guiding them toward reasonable personal goals and by supporting them in their efforts to become whatever they are capable of becoming." (p.6)

"Learning depends on *emotional state*, which determines to what we pay attention and what we learn. ...Without question, emotions are linked to attitude, motivation, persistence, perseverance, and self-worth. Thus, emotion drives personal qualities that dramatically affect a student's success or failure at school. " (p.32)

"Although emotions can overpower cognition, they can also enhance learning. 'We remember only those things we feel something about whether the feeling is fear, hunger, or desire' (Dozier, 1998)." (p. 33)

"Emotions, not cognitive stimulation, serve as the mind's primary architect for constructing its highest capacities: intelligence, morality, and sense of self (Greenspan, 1997)." (p. 34)

Social System

- Social skills govern our interactions, collaboration, and communications with others.

- Through group membership, teamwork, and team accomplishments we acquire the skills needed to work with all types of people.

- The level of effectiveness is crucial to increasing long-term productivity and vision.

- By learning how to respect the productivity and attention of others, our interactions and interpersonal skills will improve.

- When students are considered a community of learners, they learn to build on the strength of working in pairs to problem-solve, to help integrate all five of the learning systems.

The natural propensities of this system are the desires to belong to a group, to be respected, and to enjoy the attention of others.

The tendency to associate, establish links, live side by side, and cooperate is an essential characteristic of humans (Panksepp, 1998).

Below are some quotes to help orient the reader to the work of Barbara Given on this natural learning system.

Classroom and school norms take on extremely important roles regarding the development of socially acceptable behavior and in learning how to resolve conflicts. School needs to be a place where children get to know one another at a deep level. (p. 43)

Voice recognition, social mis/trust, relationships (family, peer), nurturing, behavior and play are all important in this system.

Teachers need to consider opportunities for collaboration, decision making and problem-solving with students. (p. 7) For example:

- Allow 3 minutes to work in pairs: List as many ways you can think, of how animals move from one place to another. (p. 57)

- Allow10 minutes to work in pairs: Select a fairy tale character who committed a dastardly deed, and draft a "Wanted" poster. (p.57)

Physical System

- Responsible for distributing information and prompting action throughout the brain, and body.

- Gathers information through all senses to directs us and where our body is in space.

- Physical encoding and engagement promotes connection and ownership.

- Takes longer to establish, however sustained — for example learning how to ride a bike.

- Learning is enhanced by being actively involved and by hands-on work.

- Movement and active practicing encourages the brain to work better.

- Teachers can act as a coach to teach students how to regulate their nervous system with a sensory diet that works for them.

Sensory Integration   The physical system is integral to how we process all input, through our senses. This is the juncture where our external form (our body) integrates with the cognitive system, emotional system (our mind), and the world around us. The physical system acts as a vehicle that entices and/or generates activity in the social system as well as the reflective system. These inputs come through the same sense, but may "read" or be "received" with a different level of attention due to the context from which they are derived.

As Barbara Given so aptly states in her book on the natural learning systems, the physical and behavioral aspects of the emotional systems become linked when stimulated by sensory input such as sight, sound, smell, or other sensory experiences. All within a very short period of time, our emotional response to the timing of these events influence our actions and reactions. We use background knowledge and past emotions to filter the sensory input, which results in physiological changes simultaneously throughout the brain and body. These changes help us determine what is worthy of additional attention, focused energy, and meaningful engagement amidst the bombarding information. (p. 19, 20)

Input Regulation

Karen Gouze and Karen Smith provide further context to reflect on the sensory-sensitive child in their book on practical solutions for out-of-bounds behavior as follows. The ability to regulate our nervous system is dependent on how well we are able to filter sensory input, organize, interpret, and then ultimately choose how and when to act upon it. We are constantly adapting to the world around us on a moment-to-moment basis. We experience the world through the conscious awareness of sight, hearing, smell, taste, touch, and the unconscious monitoring of balance/movement (vestibular) and body position (proprioceptive). A well-balanced sensory diet enables students to use their abilities to greater advantage... to anticipate and therefore avoid trouble, to more easily relax when needed, or to be attentionally available for learning in the classroom.

For a student to be self-directed in the classroom, they need to be able to understand their disposition in the setting, grasp where they are, and understand what is expected of them. This knowledge contributes to the student's success, failure, or somewhere in between on the continuum. Challenges often appear when students broach unfamiliar territory or if tasks become too complicated or overwhelming.

Tactual and Kinesthetic Learning

It is important for students to "do" things and to engage, if the learning process is to reap full potential. Though some students shy away from tactual (hands-on) and kinesthetic (movement and act-oriented) learning, others find learning enjoyable only when these modalities are engaged.

The following two quotes are from Barbara Given's book on natural learning systems. "...reaching out for exploration and learning by touching is tactual; and it comprises a large portion of the brain, including much of the "motor strip," as well as complex neural networks that connect the eyes, hands, and cerebellum. Some children lack eye-hand coordination and find the use of small muscles for holding a pencil and writing difficult." (p. 93)

Sensory Integration Dysfunction

"Some children demonstrate early, persistent awkwardness in gross-motor skills when they move their arms, legs, torso, hands, and feet. They appear clumsy when playing with other children their age; and they have difficulty learning to skip, jump rope, throw or catch a ball, or sometimes peddling a tricycle or riding a scooter. Some children have no difficulties with gross-motor activities associated with kinesthetic learning, but they demonstrate difficulties with the manual dexterity necessary for writing and fine-motor movement. Being strong or weak in one area does not predict the same in the other, because different brain areas are involved." (p. 94)

For some students, modulating sensory input can produce an out-of-sync response resulting in hypersensitivities such as to touching particular objects or textures, the sense of being touched, strong smells, or certain sounds. They can become anxious and/or resistant due to the over-stimulation and therefore cannot discriminate where and how the information is coming from. Over time if these problems persist, they can interfere with fine motor development, early learning skills, or appropriate social behavior. The notion of "praxis", otherwise known as motor planning, can also be affected. Basic physical and mental skills can become impaired which can cause delays in learning of self-care tasks, learning abstract or symbolic cognition such as the alphabet, organization or materials management, graphomotor issues, and/or challenges with appropriate awareness and interpretation of nonverbal or social cues.

Vestibular System Critical to learning - when children are taught specific exercises to improve balance and movement, their learning improves (Hannaford, 95). By being aware of our sensory system and what it needs, we can better prepare and ready all students for learning. Using simple and non-time consuming strategies and tools can enhance a student's ability to regulate the quality and quantity of the sensory input during the pre-learning phase and throughout instruction to receive, process, retain, or retrieve information. In short, by preparing the student's brain for learning, we are optimizing their chances for success before they take a test, listen to directions, or take notes during a lecture. For example:

- Drawing large "lazy 8's" (infinity) with outstretched arms (crossing the midline of the body) can make a dramatic difference in reading fluency (p. 95).

- Read for 1 minute. Draw large "lazy 8's" on board, reciting one letter of the alphabet at each intersection. Read for 1 more minute. Count the number of words for each reading (usually 20% more 2nd time).

- Develop Task Cards for learning state capitals, vocabulary, information within categories or conceptual arenas, etc.

Reflective System

- Responsible for weighing the past, present, and future projections.

- We interpret verbal and nonverbal cues via meta-cognition to monitor situations and to make decisions about our performance.

- When we understand what to do under a given set of circumstances, our understanding and knowing ourselves is increased.

- In consideration through self-monitoring, and the analysis of one's own learning process and acquired knowledge we understand our own learning style.

Without this system, the other four systems can produce only limited results. This refers to the personal consideration of one's own learning... achievements, failures, what worked, what didn't and what needs improvement. Below are some quotes to help orient the reader to the work of Barbara Given on this natural learning system.

"Knowledge of one's individual learning style, and learning how to use style preferences can produce great academic gain. Without explicit instruction in self-monitoring and performance analysis, this system can go dreadfully underdeveloped." (p. 9)

We need to teach students reflective thinking and meta-cognition deliberately, in a consistent manner, until students internalize the process.(p.122)

Reflective Learning depends on basic input from our senses and internal viscera, as well as complex memory systems, numerous brain structures, pathways, networks and subsystems. The frontal lobes are perhaps the most critical, acting as massive inhibitors and shapers of primary urges (aggression, violence, sexual activity). They allow us to anticipate, plan, balance and control emotions, and maintain a sense of ourselves as contributors toward our future well-being.

This system weighs past, present, and probable thoughts and behaviors, then predicts future outcomes by asking self-directed questions.

Example   *Across All Learning "Systems"*

"Take the chance meeting of a student and a teacher. Neurotransmitters rapidly signal neurons associated with each of the systems to fire or not to fire - say this and keep quiet about that. The cognitive system recalls the person's name, what class they have in common, and the expectations established during that class yesterday. The emotional system re-experiences a measure of anxiety or pleasure depending on the conditions of their previous interactions. The student does not ask about the homework, for instance, if it is not completed. The social system provides standards of conduct: make eye contact, exchange polite "hellos", ask about the upcoming school-wide celebration. Inhibitory neurons of the physical system keep them standing in proximity long enough for quick exchanges before the excitatory neurons stimulate movement for them to part. This all takes place in moments. Later, when the student or teacher tells another about the encounter, the reflective system relives those moments mentally and ponders: "I wonder if I said too much about my friends" or "I wish it hadn't been right when I felt in a rush to get to a phone call." (p.9-10 w/ revision)

Source: "Teaching to the Brain's Natural Learning Systems", Barbara K. Given, ASCD, 2002

SECTION FOUR *Robert Marzano et. al. Nine Best Strategies*

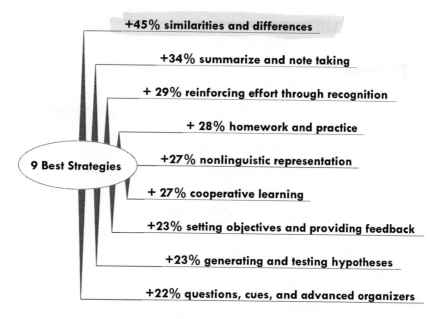

+45% similarities and differences

+34% summarize and note taking

+ 29% reinforcing effort through recognition

+ 28% homework and practice

+27% nonlinguistic representation

+ 27% cooperative learning

+23% setting objectives and providing feedback

+23% generating and testing hypotheses

+22% questions, cues, and advanced organizers

9 Best Strategies

About the same time as Barbara Given's important work, came a meta-analysis of educational research and best practices by Marzano, Pickering and Pollock (ASCD 2001). These careful researchers surveyed educational studies over the past 35 years, culling out those that did not meet rigorous standards of validity and reliability criteria. The remaining studies fell into nine categories. In brief, they are depicted in the following chart.

These nine categorical strategies are more closely aligned with student achievement outcomes than other researched approaches. As such, they provide a useful template for designing lessons and units of study. It is apparent to the authors that the successful merging of the brain's natural learning systems with the most effective researched instructional strategies must become the work of practitioners interested in improving the quality of the learning experience as well as the resultant outcomes. This book will make use of many of the nine strategies outlined by Marzano, Pikering, and Pollock in their 2001 work with a focus on one of the nine, Nonlinguistic Representations. In providing several methods for implementing instructional activities within this strategy, many, if not most of the other eight strategies are also utilized, as you will see in the ensuing activities and approaches.

Marzano et. al.'s work on the nine strategies is defined, summarized and briefly outlined as follows.

Strategy ~ 1 *Similarities and Differences*

Definition	Having learners identify or explore how things are similar or different is the most effective strategy relating to student achievement outcomes.
Comparison	The process of identifying similarities and differences between or among things or ideas.
Classification	The process of organizing things into categories based on similar characteristics, noting the parameters of inclusion in each category and reasons for them being grouped together.
Metaphor	The process of identifying a basic pattern in one area or topic and relating it to another area or topic that is different, but follows the same basic pattern. The topics connect by abstract or nonlinear relationship.
Analogy	The process of identifying relationships between pairs of concepts, for example: relationships between relationships.

Research **+45% impact on student performance outcomes**

- There are several ways to frame this strategy. Four are reviewed and defined below.

- Instructor teaches similarities/differences explicitly, identifying important items.

- Students identify similarities/differences on their own

- Teacher provides (or asks students to generate) graphic/symbolic representations of similarities/differences.

- Variations of similarities/differences can be used as in comparing, classifying, metaphor and analogy.

Strategy ~ 2 *Summarizing and Note Taking*

Summarizing Defined

The process of selecting what to keep, delete, or alter. Keep main ideas. Delete trivia and redundancy. Alter common terms into a category.

Note Taking Defined

The central component of Summarization.

Research

+34% impact on student performance outcomes

- Explicit practice with instructor demonstration can prove to be very effective.

- When students capture essential notes from an essay, it is helpful that they understand its information structure. For example: how an introduction or summary is constructed and why, the use of tense, or phrasing strategies.

- Templates with "rule-based" strategies frames can be key in enabling students to capture the important information.

- Note-worthy information can be derived from many forms: narrative, specific illustration, definition, argument, problem/solution, or conversation.

- Using reciprocal teaching techniques such as summarizing, questioning, clarifying, or predicting can also serve as productive note taking tools.

- Verbatim note taking is NOT effective.

- Remind your students that notes are a work in progress to be reviewed, reorganized, and referenced, and that they too provide feedback and reflection.

- Quantity of notes is more effective than efficiency of notes.

Notes Strategies

- Informal Outline: focus on major ideas and related details.

- Clustering, webbing, or mind mapping: encircling main ideas in a nonlinear manner, drawing lines to related information, the use of color to organize like information, or illustrations to tell stories.

- Templates: prepared nonlinguistic forms to support the collection and organization of information and related detail.

23

Strategy ~ 3 *Reinforcing Effort and Providing Recognition*

Defined   Learners attribute success based on their ability, their effort, other people, and/or plain old luck. If they are to sustain action toward achievement, they need to be encouraged to understand. Often, this determines the outcome, and the effort put forth can play a substantial role in intrinsic motivation.

Reinforcing   Explicitly noting the connection between student effort as equally important to the achievement of desired outcomes.

Recognition   Paying attention to, articulating and/or rewarding cause and effect links between achieved outcomes and previous efforts.

Research   **+29% impact on student performance outcomes**

- Linking outcomes to specific performance goals enhances intrinsic motivation, with either abstract recognition or with tangible tokens.

- Abstract symbolic recognition is more effective than the use of tangible rewards.

- Rewards and praise can serve to diminish desire when intrinsic motivation was initially in place.

Strategy ~ 4 *Homework and Practice*

Defined   Homework extends learning opportunities beyond official school day time.

Homework Goal   To provide high-quality, specific feedback, in a timely manner (very soon!).

Practice Goal   To master a skill and increase conceptual understanding.

Research   **+28% impact on student performance outcomes**

- The amount assigned should vary (increase) with age. Homework is more effective for older students.

  - Grades 4-6 = 5%
  - Grades 7-9 = 12%
  - Grades 10-12 = 24%

- Parent involvement with homework should be kept to a minimum.

- The purpose of homework must be clearly articulated.

- Practice homework has a high degree of student familiarity, providing focused practice on a skill or knowledge set.

- Elaboration homework seeks to prepare for a new concept or to extend content that has already been introduced. Understanding the principles underpinning knowledge is essential.

- If assigned, homework must be graded (+28%), and preferably commented on (+30%) or the value diminishes greatly.

- Homework environment: consistent, organized place; consistent time or schedule; sufficient prompts and encouragement; cease at a specific time, whether done or not.

- Varied approaches to homework enhance motivation/interest.

- Students may share in tracking or scoring some homework.

Strategy ~ 5 *Nonlinguistic Representation*

Defined   Knowledge is "stored" in two forms, linguistic and imagery (Pavio, 1990), which results in enhanced memory and recall.

Research   **+27% impact on student performance outcomes**

- Variety of ways to accomplish the production of imagery in minds (NLRs)

  ○ Graphic representations created on paper or other medium.

  ○ Physical Models: commonly thought of as manipulatives or ways to engage learners in concrete representations of the idea, info, skill, pattern or process.

  ○ Mental Pictures: Symbolic of the construct being learned, ways to help learners "feel" or consider circumstances regarding the topic/situation.

  ○ Drawing and pictographs: Mind mapping, a la Buzan, or Clustering a la Rico - symbolic images/drawings that represent relationship, meaning, or importance relative to other factors or information.

  ○ Kinesthetics: Using physical movement or positioning to demonstrate or replicate an idea, context or flow of activity.

- Nonlinguistic Representations should elaborate knowledge, devising mental models to approximate concrete forms.

Strategy ~ 6 *Cooperative Learning*

Defined   Placing learners together in various size groups to interact. Cooperative Learning activities engage the social learning system to enhance processing, strengthening attention and improving recall.

Research   **+27% impact on student performance outcomes**

- Students of all ability levels benefit from grouping when compared with no grouping at all. In other words, working together in like or dissimilar ability groups is advantageous to working alone.

- Promotes positive interdependence (we're in this together).

- Fosters accountability (both individual and group - contributions toward goals).

- Interactive postures (working to help each other, supporting effort and success).

- Group processing (reflecting on performance and how to prove). Interpersonal skills (decision making, trust, leadership, communication, etc.).

- More effective than working and competing as individuals.

- Group size should be kept relatively small (2-4).

- Grouping practices are more effective when used at least once per week.

Strategy ~ 7 *Setting Objectives and Providing Feedback*

Defined   Goal setting is the act of establishing direction for learning through identifying target objectives or outcomes. In the classroom, these usually reflect what the student must know and be able to do as a result of the lesson or unit of study.

Feedback refers to efforts or items that provide students with information regarding their current performance.

Research   **+23% impact on student performance outcomes**

- Instructional goals narrow the general focus, but should not be too specific.
- Students should be encouraged to personalize the overall goals set by the teacher.
- Hattie (1992) "The most powerful single modification that enhances achievement is feedback. The simplest prescription for improving education must be "dollops of feedback."
- Telling "right" or "wrong" has a negligible effect if done after each item.
- Best: explain what is accurate and what is inaccurate.
- Feedback must be timely--immediate or day after.
- Feedback needs to be criteria specific, informing students where they stand relative to a specific knowledge or skill component.
- Feedback can be provided by students, themselves and/or with classmates.
- Rubrics can be especially useful for providing more feedback than a single number or score.

Strategy ~ 8 *Generating and Testing Hypothesis*

Defined   Applying knowledge to a new or varied circumstance to predict an effect.

Research   **+23% impact on student performance outcomes**

- Either inductive or deductive approaches are useful.

- Clearly articulating and writing a prediction helps to clarify understanding.

- Problem solving, investigation, observation, invention and inquiry are often components used in testing hypotheses.

- Committing to a prediction or hypothesis helps to anchor connections in the brain - to create stronger processing potential that is longer lived.

Strategy ~ 9.1 *Questions, Cues, and Advanced Organizers*

Definition   Questions and Cues help students retrieve and/or use what they know (prior knowledge). Cues "hint" and questions elicit what students already know about a topic or idea. Questioning and cueing account for as much as 80% of classroom activities.

Research   **+22% impact on student performance outcomes**

- Questions/Cues should focus on what is important, not on the unusual or the "interesting." The more students know about a topic, the more interested they'll be.

- Higher level questions produce more long term memory and understanding than lower level questions. Questions requiring learners to analyze produce more learning than questions that request simple recall.

- "Wait Times"... a brief period of waiting before accepting responses affects the depth of student verbal offerings.

  ° 1st wait time: time that takes place after the teacher asks a question or otherwise prompts the class.

  ° 2nd wait time: time that takes place after a student responds - before the teacher says any remark.

- Questions are also effective when asked prior to a lesson/activity, establishing a mental set or context for what is to follow.

- Analytic questions cause students to critique information.

- Analyze Errors:

  ° What information shows errors in reasoning?

  ° Does the information mislead? Is it incomplete?

  ° How could it be improved/more accurate?

- Construct Support:

  ° What argument would support the claim made?

  ° What limitations are evident or assumptions made?

- Analyze Perspectives:

  ° Why is this (statement/information) good/bad/neutral?

  ° What reasoning do you have for your assertion?

  ° What other perspective may be viable? Why?

Strategy ~ 9.2 *Questions, Cues, and Advanced Organizers*

Definition   Advanced Organizers introduce relevant introductory material used in advance of targeted learning, and are presented at the concept/abstract levels of generality and inclusiveness. They provide initial scaffolding upon which following information/ideas may be more easily placed or retained. Advanced Organizers may seek to bridge what a learner knows, needs to know and will be encountering soon.

Research   **+22% impact on student performance outcomes, depending on type**

- Advanced Organizers should focus on what is important, not unusual.

- Advanced Organizers should address "higher order" contexts and concepts for optimal impact.

- Advanced Organizers work best with information that is not organized (the intent of their use is to "organize" thinking)... thus they address things prior to a structure or organization being applied).

- Advanced Organizers differ in type or use, in effect size as follows:

Graphic Organizers +20%
Nonlinguistic representations of information, categorized or ordered prior to instruction. Students gain a "feel" for the relationship of parts-to-wholes relationships.

Narrative +20%
Information presented in story format, personalized being the most effective. For example: hearing a story about or from someone directly involved in a hurricane prior to studying about weather/storms.

Expository +29%
Describes new content students are about to engage in. Provides key ideas/categories of information prior to student exposure to more in-depth information.

Skimming +26%
A casual review of information prior to reading in depth or engaging in an activity. For example: view solar maps prior to a planetarium visit.

SECTION FIVE *Bi-Modal Imagery & the Brain*

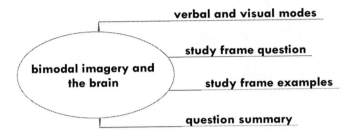

As a people with vested interested in building independent learners, the verbal skills of reading and writing have held the top spot in our efforts to advance student capacities, access to further learning, and even increased scores on standardized measures. Clearly, verbal skills are enormously important and play a leading role in establishing one's ability to prosper across several domains. Even so, there are other "sides" to learning. For some time now, we have developed discussions and jargon around such topics as learning styles, multiple intelligences and other alternatives to the steady diet that verbal modes utilize. Important to the brain and how it operates to form memory, is "often not emphasized..." the visual side.

Visual aspects of brain processing have often been relegated to an association with sight. Though we understand that stimuli received through the eyes and processed in the visual cortex are a major source of input to the world about us, we may overlook a powerful factor in memory building capacity. In a study reported in the <u>Nature 2004 Journal</u> by Weliky, electrodes were placed into the visual cortex of ferrets. As they were presented with visual stimuli, only 20% of the brain activity came from the external visual stimuli, while 80% of the activity in the brain was "internally driven." From this we are compelled to consider the vast amount of activity in the brain that occurs in a visual mode. Linking verbal components of learning with this reservoir of potential appears to be a vital source of anchoring brain activity for sustained memory.

The work of Steven Koslyn, at Harvard and the Massachusetts General Hospital, also notes the array of brain activity occurring through external visual stimuli in accompaniment with internal, perceptual imagery. The image below illustrates the areas of the brain (in metaphoric representation) that activate upon externally sighted imagery. We've all learned that as visual information enters the brain it is first interpreted in the occipital lobe to the rear of the cranium. However, in rapid cascade, the inputs stimulate multiple modules in all brain lobes. Thus, when we "see" something, we are enacting past, present and future potentials that all come to bear on our ultimate perception of the items we are addressing.

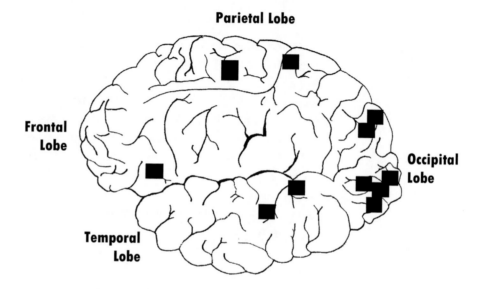

Figure 2: The Brain and Areas of Bi-Modal Activity

Kosslyn suggests that we have natural capacities to generate, inspect and transform images in our mind. For instance, if you are not in your home and try to remember how many windows are in your bedroom, you can precisely recall this. Therefore, you can "generate" visual recall that is very accurate even if you are not in proximity to the actual visual inputs. Next, you can "inspect" items in your mind and generate discrete levels of detail. If asked to recall what type of locks are on the windows in your bedroom, you can also do this. In your mind, you zero in on a window and "see" the lock. Additionally, we can move objects in our minds without benefit of having them in front of us or physically manipulating them. Try this. With your eyes closed, think of the capitol letter "N" in your mind. If you rotate it counterclockwise ninety degrees (a quarter turn to the left), what do you now have/see? (The letter "Z")

Many authors and researchers have contributed to this work, leading to dual coding theory or DCT (Pavio, Sadoski, Rieber, Tzeng, Tribble, Chu). Dual coding theory provides a model for understanding how the brain codes information. "Memory packets" have two modes; linguistic and nonlinguistic. In essence, our system for storing information for later use and application is comprised of verbal elements and visual elements. Bi-modal packets are just that - bimodal. They have two separate but complimentary facets that, in combination, provide a greater capacity for constructing stronger, more durable, and more accessible memory sets. It makes little sense to focus on the process of creating memory if we don't give equal voice to the act of cueing memory for recall and use at later times.

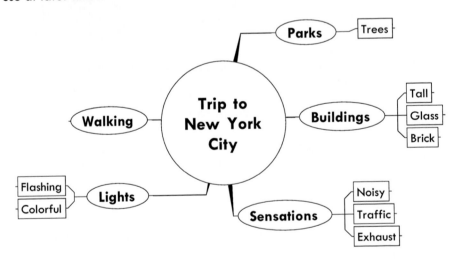

Figure 3: Bi-Modal Packets and Effective Processing of Information: Initial Exposure to a Topic, Experience, or Idea

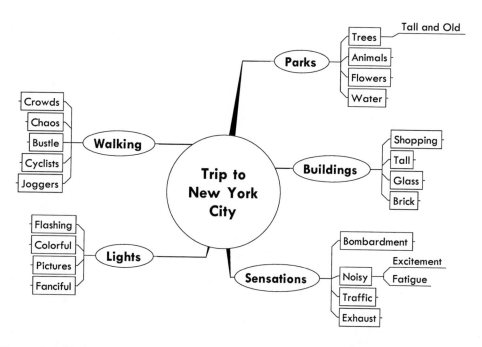

Figure 4: Added Details in a Generalized Form of "Background Knowledge"

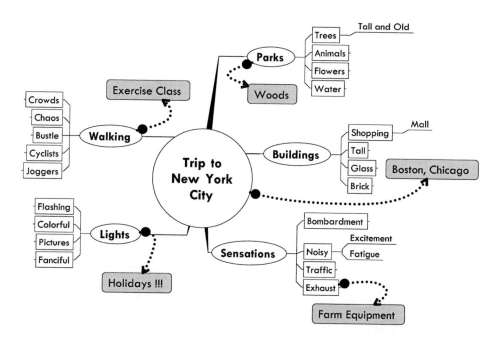

Figure 5: Elaboration of Ideas to New Categories or Other Personal Experiences

Study Frame Question   *If we frame memory/recall in the bimodal context and ask the following questions:*

"Which situation would likely produce more understanding, more durable links and greater recall? What order would you place these options in (from most recall to least)?"

- Text without pictures (words/verbal mode only).
- Text with pictures (words, with pictures provided in the text or by the teacher).
- Text accompanied by reader generated imagery.
- Text accompanied by reader generated imagery as well as text/teacher provided pictures.

Below are several studies. Review each as a means to determining your response to the questions above. Pertinent information is provided with each, along with the finding(s).

Study Frame ~ 1   *Impact on Memory of Illustrated vs. Non-Illustrated Story Text*

Subjects   Community college students

Activity   Students read a 2100 word story

- Students were provided imagery reports immediately and 48 hours after the completion of the reading.
- Student reports varied in type by categories of reports by paragraph, elaborated beyond paragraph, across paragraphs & reader-originated.

Assessment Method   Text (questions) as well as by recall of imagery.

Findings   Verbal recall declined after 48-hour delay. Imagery reports did not.

Authors   Sadoski, Goetz, Olivarez, Lee & Roberts (1990)

Study Frame ~ 2 *Impact on Degree of Importance, Emotional Response, & Degree of Spontaneous Imagery on Recall*

Subjects   University undergraduates

Activity   Students read a 2100 word story

- Students read literary short stories and articles from magazines.

- Students numerically rated each paragraph for:

  ° Degree of imagery experiences the paragraph induced

  ° Degree of emotional response the paragraph elicited

  ° Importance of the paragraph as they perceived it

Assessment Method   Questions asked of all, as well as by their reported recall of imagery.

Findings
- There was a correlation between imagery and emotional response ratings.

- Sixteen days later, student recall on highly rated imagery and emotion paragraphs was high.

- Recall on paragraphs that students rated highly "important" was much lower than paragraphs rated highly emotional or with high levels of induced imagery.

Authors   Sadoski, Goetz, & Kangiser (1988)

Study Frame ~ 3 *Explicitly Taught Mental Imagery*

Subjects Students of grades 1 & 3

Activity Students were asked to read short segments of stories

- The Imagery group was told to make pictures in their heads to help them remember.

- The Control group was told to think about what they read, in order to remember.

- After each reading segment, the students of both groups were asked, "What do you think is going to happen next?"

Assessment Method Student responses to the question were scored for factual accuracy and number (quantity) of predictions.

Findings

- The 3rd grade Imagery group reported twice as many facts and predictions as the Control group.

- The 1st grade Imagery group outperformed Controls on both measures, but not to a significant level.

- The researcher speculated that the burden of verbal processing may inhibit simultaneous formation of images. Very beginning readers may do better reading and forming images successively (read segment, form image, read segment, form image, etc.).

Authors Gambrell (1982)

Study Frame ~ 4   *Explicitly Taught Mental Imagery*

Subjects   Students of grade three

Activity
- Imagery group: Students in the Imagery group were given practice in forming mental images from sentences and paragraphs.

- Control group: Students in the Control group were provided examples of good images derived from the passages.

- Both groups read a 950 word story with alternating printed and blank pages.

- The Imagery group was reminded regularly to form mental images at each blank page.

- The Control group was reminded regularly to recall as much as they could from the text.

- There was no difference in the reading times provided for the passages.

Assessment Method   24 short-answer items administered as a test.

Findings
- Imagery group significantly outperformed the Control group.

Authors   Pressley (1976)

Study Frame ~ 5 *Mental Imagery Training and Comprehension*

Subjects   4th & 5th grade poor readers

Activity
- **Imagery Group**   A short training session, encouraging students to make pictures in their head while reading, was provided to the Imagery study group.

- **Control Group** The Control group was told to do whatever they could while they were reading to understand and remember the reading passages.

- The reading passages included both explicit and implicit inconsistencies embedded in the text.

- Students in both groups were instructed to determine if there was anything that was not clear or easy to understand in the passage.

Assessment Method   Students were asked to identify explicit and implicit inconsistencies in text passages.

Findings   The Imagery group identified both types of inconsistencies (explicit and implicit) more than twice as often as the Control group.

Few of the Control group students reported using any imagery in their approaches to the understanding and recall of the passages as they read.

Authors   Gambrell & Bales (1986)

Study Frame ~ 6   *Induced Mental Imagery, Provided Story Illustrations, Un-illustrated Text and Comprehension*

Subjects   120 4th grade students

Activity   Read a 925 word basal reader story

- 4 groups were formed

1.	**Control Group**	"Read carefully and try to remember as much as you can". This activity is using un-illustrated text.
2.	**Imagery Group**	"Read and form your own mental images (un-illustrated text)."
3.	**Illustrations Group**	"Read and pay attention to the five text-relevant story illustrations that are provided".
4.	**Imagery/Illustration Group**	"Read, form your own images and pay attention to the five text-relevant story illustrations that are provided."

Assessment Method   Comprehension and recall passages administered

Findings

- The Imagery/Illustration group, asked to form their own images and attend to the provided illustrations, significantly outperformed all others on measures of comprehension and recall.

- The Imagery group, asked to form their own images,-- outperformed the Illustrations-only group on recall of story structure elements, as well as complete story recall.

- Control group #1 had the lowest performance on all measured recall tasks - even though *they were the only group instructed to read to remember.*

Authors   Gambrell & Jawitz (1993)

Study Frame ~ 7 *Concreteness of Language and Recall*

Subjects   University undergraduates

Activity 1   Students read simple declarative sentences either with or without concrete modifiers. For example:

- "The set fell off the table" vs.

- "The ivory chess set fell off the table."

Activity 2   Students read simple declarative sentences with either concrete or abstract modifiers. For example:

- "The oil-pressure gauge was covered with dust."

- vs. "The gauge was covered with dust."

Assessment Method   Number of sentences recalled.

Findings   ▪   Participants remembered 50% more of the sentences with concrete modifiers in both activities.

Authors   Anderson (1974)

Study Frame ~ 8   *Effects of Concreteness on Familiarity, Comprehensibility, Interestingness, and Immediate and Delayed Recall of Sentences and Paragraphs*

Subjects   University undergraduates

Activity   Students read text on historical figures who varied in familiarity (a panel of experts was used to determine levels of familiarity).

- Texts were made either more concrete or more abstract.

Assessment Method   Student ratings of text on comprehension, familiarity and interest levels.

Findings
- Concrete text was rated more comprehensible and interesting than abstract text, though not as more familiar.
- Concrete texts were recalled 2-5 times better than abstract tests, both immediately and five days afterward.
- Placing a concrete sentence before an abstract sentence about the same historical figure increased recall of the abstract sentence by 70%.

Authors   Sadoski, Goetz & Fritz (1993)

43

Final Study Summary   *Imagery vs. Concreteness*

The final two studies focused on issues that did not directly assess "imagery" as a term brought to the attention of the subjects. However, "concreteness" in text is thought to naturally elicit more imagery activity than "abstractions" would, thus the link to mental imagery. Overall, the eight studies cited above were conducted over two decades and with various ages of participants.

There appears to be common ground that speaks to the questions posed:

- Which situation would likely produce more understanding, produce the most durable links, and gain the greatest recall?

- What order would you place each option in?

Please rank them in terms of most recall to least:

- Text without pictures (words/verbal mode only).

- Text with pictures (words, with pictures provided in the text or by the teacher).

- Text accompanied by reader generated imagery.

- Text accompanied by reader generated imagery as well as text/teacher provided pictures.

The order of impact, based on dual coding theory and the studies above would suggest that when readers actively form mental imagery and also have access to pictures, their level of recall and understanding increases. The surprising finding is that readers actively forming mental images while reading outperform readers with text only or with text and pictures provided.

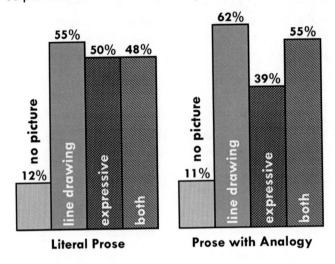

Figure 5: Effects of Illustration & Analogy on Written Prose Recall

Credit: Hayes, David A.; Henk, William A.

Facilitative Effects of Analogies and Illustrations on Understanding and Remembering Written Directions. Paper presented at the Annual Meeting of the American Educational Research Association (Montreal Canada, April 1983)

SECTION SIX *Nonlinguistic Representation Activities*

Sensory Activities

Mental Activities

Visual ~ 1   Organization: Venn to Criteria

Compare and Contrast

Student Generated

Students sort, form categories and determine reasons for inclusion. The reasons for grouping become the criteria for a given category that can lead to description or ultimately, definition.

Frame the Assignment

1.   Provide a list of items.

- Characters from novels/books the class has read; people studied through history; animals; plant life; etc. For example:

Jennifer   Alice   Harry   Homer   Johnson   Amad   Jorge   Niel

Contrasting categories against which students will assess items causes processing in the brain.

2.   Provide students with a dichotomy for each circle of the Venn diagram. For example:

- Good / Bad
- Popular / Unpopular
- Quadrilateral / Non-quadrilateral

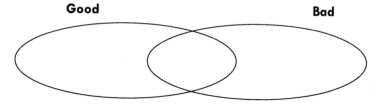

Good   **Bad**

Exploring similarities and differences are the #1 way to enhance student achievement.

3.   As individuals, ask students to place items from the list you have provided into the Venn diagram (note: you may or may not want to also include the overlapping area that depicts characteristics of both sides) according to the dichotomy you established. Students consider how each entry is alike or different as it relates to the contrasting categories.

4.   Ask students to form pairs or triads and discuss their placement of each item. As they confer with each other, ask them to generate a list of reasons why they have placed items in one circle vs. the other. See example below.

Social Learning System. Having students commit on paper, as well as articulate ideas.

Good   **Both / Neutral**   **Bad**

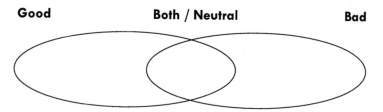

Reasons	**Reasons**	**Reasons**
1. Told Truth	1. Didn't Get Involved	1. Hurt Alice
2. Stood Up for Neil	2. Only Did it Once	2. Lied
3. Helped another	3.	3. Stole

- Discuss where the group placed the items in the Venn diagram.
- Make note of the differences (if any) for future discussion.

Further refinement of thinking regarding categories and themes.

5. Discuss the list of reasons in each category (good, bad, neutral) and ask the students if they notice any consistency or trends.

- These become the criteria for inclusion in a category and can serve to help describe a characteristic or group, or to define a person, thing or other item.

Visual ~ 2   Organization: Multiple Venn Categories

Categorization

Student Generated

Students sort and form categories from multiple items as a means to better understand subgroups within an extensive list of items.

Begin a new body of knowledge or set of skills with learners by providing context

1.   Provide a list of items.

   ▪ Animals in general; events in history; characters in a book; formulas; etc. For example:

Spider	Bass	Blue Jay	Beaver	Fox	Sheep	Starfish
Cow	Monkey	Squirrel	Lobster	Horse	Ostrich	Camel
Ant	Snake	Ladybug	Snail	Squid	Whale	Elephant
Goldfish	Clam	Robin	Porpoise	Pig	Parrott	Mosquito
Frog	Turtle	Sparrow				

Social Learning System

Students generate their own categories.

2.   Ask students to take 3-5 minutes and work in pairs to create groupings of animals that have a likeness. For this purpose, use each animal only once - even though it may "fit" into more than one category. As they form groupings of animals, have them give the grouping a name or title.

Example of student groupings with headings.

Fly	**Four Legs**	**Live in Water**	**Shell**
Blue Jay	Horse	Porpoise	Snail
Parrott	Pig	Whale	Clam
Robin	Camel	Starfish	Turtle
Sparrow	Elephant		

Similarities and differences are the #1 way to enhance student achievement.

3.   Ask the pairs of students to share their "headings" or titles for the groups they formed. As they offer them, write them on the board for all to see. After all have been offered, tell the class that these are categories they have developed with a criteria for inclusion. For example: fly; four legs; live in water; have a shell, etc.

Setting up a unit of study with concept development prior to content exploration.

4.   Ask students if some animals could be placed in multiple groups or categories. Discuss some possibilities. Also ask students if some categories could be joined or grouped. This is the beginning of understanding how things are alike/different - or - what they have in common or the differences between them.

Setting up a unit of study with concept development prior to content exploration.

5.   Converge on the focus of your unit (mammals, reptiles, insects, indo-skeletal creatures, etc). Students now have a board context, from which the focus of their studies can be drawn.

Visual ~ 3 Organization: Theme Investigation

Developing distinctions within a Theme

Exploring themes and essential concepts through eras in time or across disciplines serves to anchor main ideas and foster transfer for future learning.

Teacher Generated

Present a major, transferable topic

Modeling a process before expecting others to use it (Teacher generated prior to student generated)

1. Supply an image or question that frames the "investigation" you would like the class to undertake, such as:

    ▪ "Here is a hammer. In what ways does this represent a powerful "technology" that changed the world?"

    ▪ Student generated option:

        o Sometimes, to establish the process, you can start with a teacher generated focus (hammer example) and then evolve to a student generated example.

        o This serves to model the process so that students understand what is expected of them.

Social Learning System

2a. Ask students to form pairs or triads and generate a list of ideas that respond to the question posed (5 minutes).

2b. Once this is accomplished, ask them to explore alternative or opposite reasons why something may or may not be so (5 minutes).

Possibilities from a broad spectrum will generate a more thorough discussion of important aspects

3. POST words regarding your theme about the room – you will need enough for about the class size divided by 3 or 4. For example:

    ▪ If the class has 24 students (divided by 3 or 4) you'd need about 6-8 items.

        o Take time to discuss/explain any items that may potentially cause confusions. The students need not fully comprehend all items to complete this activity, but basic knowledge is important.

Human Genome	Hammer	Microchips	Printing Press
Atomic Reaction	Clock	Railroads	Laser
Automobile	Rope	Microwave	FMRI
Aircraft	Television	Radio	Computer
Pharmaceuticals	Wheel	Combustion Engine	

Overarching concepts create comparative thinking that causes more processing.	4. Provide an essential question, such as: ■ "Which technology has represented the largest impact on our world?" or "Which poses the largest threat?" 5. Independently, have students consider possibilities and determine their choice for most and/or least impact. Ask students to capture their understanding in a form of medium. For example: draw, illustrate, graph, write, etc.
Students move to choice based on their hypothesis and then commit via movement.	6. Ask students to get up and move to the item or word they have selected. ■ **Option 1** Stay seated, select one, and form groups. First 3 to select one make a group for that item. Others must select another item. Minimum of two students form a group. ■ **Option 2** Have students who did not get their first choice form a group and decide on the least impact item and progress with the assignment from that perspective.
Groups discuss reasons for choices and generate list. *Compare/contrast.*	7. Have students at each location discuss as a group their reasons for their choice – and list essential ideas on a piece of chart paper (if you intend to have them display their rationale), or on regular paper.
Class discusses each choice and posts reasons	8. Groups post/share their list of reasons. As a class, discuss the reasons provided and note similarities or emerging themes.
Small Groups or independent review all input. *Social Learning System*	**Options** ■ Once they are aware of all justifications and ideas for the impact technologies may have had, ask students to continue to work in small groups to re-examine all choices and select a final one. Then, construct a formal response to the question prompt, providing a comprehensive explanation of their choice. **Independently or in Small Groups** ■ Ask students to review all input provided, independent of the specific technologies and form a list of criteria to use in evaluating the impact of inventions and technologies over time and in the future. Identify categories for consideration (themes of impact).

Visual ~ 4   Organization: Theme Contrast

Constructing Themes Across Multiple Criteria

Exploring multiple inputs to unveil strands in common helps learners to link ideas and build networks for transfer.

Student Generated

Frame an investigation with an overarching concept.	**Essential or Big Question** 1. Supply an image or question that frames the "investigation" you would like the class to undertake, such as: • Which has influenced the world more, geography or technology? • Sometimes, to establish the process, you can start with a teacher generated focus and then evolve to a student-generated example, so that students understand the process and what is expected of them.
Prior knowledge engaged.	2. Student Generated Ideation Ask students to brainstorm a list of geological phenomenon and technological innovations worthy of consideration.
Possibilities from a broad spectrum will generate a more thorough discussion of important aspects	Below could be ideas that students brainstorm for consideration. You must decide if you, too, will enter any items.

Atomic Reaction	Deserts	Mountain Ranges	Oil Deposits
Rain Forests	Hammer	Railroads	Printing Press
Pharmaceuticals	Rope	Canyons	Oceans
Volcanic Activity	Television	Major Rivers	fMRI
Human Genome	Wheel	Combustion Engine	Computer

Essential question for transfer.	3. Pose the big question: • Which has influenced the world more, geography or technology? • Discuss any items that students appear confused about.
Having learners "commit" in some manner helps increase brain processing.	4. Independently, have students consider possibilities and determine which has caused more impact (geography or technology). Then have them select the item that best represents that position.

Physical learning system; commit with body in space; hypothesizing	**5.** Ask students to get up and move to the item or word they have selected. ▪ **Option:** Stay seated, select one, and form groups. **5b.** Try to get students to split into two substantial groups, one group representing geography and the other representing technology.
Social Learning System Pro/Con thesis development.	**6.** Have students in each major group divide into sub-groups based on their item selections within the category (geography or technology). Once in small groups of 2-4, have them discuss and list their reasons for their overall selection (geography or technology) and then their ideas as to why the specific item represents a good example (of why).
Main ideas and supporting details.	**7.** Sub-groups list their selection along with specific examples, and with reasons for their choices. Once posted, the class discusses each choice.
Given prior organization and exposure, learner success at assessment tasks is enhanced.	**8.** Once they are aware of all justifications and ideas for the impact technologies may have had, ask students to construct a formal written position with respect to the question prompt.
Homework/assignment: Follow up with survey of other people's views.	**9.** Have students pose the question to a parent or other teacher in the building to determine how others view the issue. Compare/contrast adult input with various student positions.

Visual ~ 5   Images: Single Image Sort

Visual - Verbal
Memory Packets

Linking the visual and verbal elements of bimodal memory packets helps learners develop memory pathways.

Teacher Generated

Visual cues provided for subsequent verbal (words) to connect to.

1.   Put an image before the class. For example:

   ▪   An overhead, photograph, or drawing.

Student generates words from their experiences.

2.   Students independently write/generate three words that come to mind from viewing the image.

3.   As a class, students offer responses, while the teacher writes on the board or chart paper.

Referencing visuals can assist the process of organizing and generating verbal outputs.

4.   As individuals or in pairs, students write about the image and their impression(s) derived from it.

Visual ~ 6 Images: Image Melt

Visual - Verbal Memory Packets

Teacher Generated

Linking the visual and verbal elements of bimodal memory packets helps learners develop memory pathways.

Similar and different stimuli are knows to create increased processing and memory

Activity 1: Different Images

1.   Place two "different" (contrasting) images before the class.

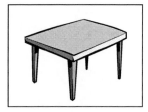 

Student generated work.

2.   Students independently write/generate three words that come to mind from viewing the image.

3.   As a class, students offer responses, while the teacher writes on the board or chart paper.

Categorizing helps learners process for understanding and classifying.

4.   As a class, students categorize words into lists. For example: synonyms or vocabulary.

Having contrasted different inputs, especially visual inputs helps learners form memory.

5.   Students write about differences (contrast).

Activity 2: Similar Images

1.   Place two "similar" images before the class.

2.   Same as above. Identify criteria for similarity and differences.

Similar items create opportunity for more subtle distinctions.

3.   Write about subtle distinctions between the similar images.

Visual ~ 7   Images: Group Image Query

Visual - Verbal Memory Packets

Identification with an image or other graphic representation, helps to conjure ideas and feelings, to which content can be sorted or added.

Teacher Generated

Visual imagery prompts brain activity

1. Post images of things about the room – you will need enough for about the class size divided by 3 or 4. For example:

    ▪ If class has 24 students, divide by 3, therefore about 8 items will be needed.

Posing essential questions focuses learner attention on important, transferable ideas.

2. Provide the concept/focus of study/question:

    ▪ "Who was the best leader?"

    ▪ "Which person was the most troubled?"

    ▪ "What was the primary cause of the revolt?"

Predicting, making choices, or hypothesizing serves to cause greater processing activity in the brain

3. Independently ask students to consider the possibilities and determine their top two choices.

Physically moving to show commitment engages the Physical Learning System as well as the Cognitive Learning System.

4. Ask students to **get up and move** to the posted image they feel is the best choice.

Social Learning System

Elaborating on reasons for selecting position.

5. Have students at each location discuss as a group their reasons for their choice – and list essential ideas on a piece of chart paper (regular paper).

6. As a class, discuss each choice and the generated reasons, listing all.

7. List all reasons on the board (independent of where the items came from).

Social Learning System

8. Have students work in small groups (pairs-triads-quads) to form a description of the concept/focus/question provided in #2.

    ▪ Note: Definitions are okay as part of the description, but the work must go beyond a simple definition to include: examples, images, descriptions of use/setting/related things, etc.

9. Have students share their work.

Visual ~ 8   Images: Compare and Contrast Chalk Talk

Compare and Contrast in Visual Stimuli

Using visual materials to help learners learn to compare and contrast inputs supports the bimodal memory packet development, which ultimately can improve recall.

Teacher Generated

Multiple visual inputs provide opportunities for reflection.

1. Place several images on the walls that capture or provoke the main idea of your lesson or objective. Place or tape chart paper nearby each image.

Restricting conventional verbal options (talking) helps the brain focus on other aspects of stimuli.

2. Have students walk about silently (no talking) for 4-5 minutes, writing thoughts and reactions to each image on paper hung near the image.

Share, synthesize ideas and share reactions.

3. As a class, discuss reactions and thoughts for each image.

Writing may be more likely and more organized when a learner has visual information to reference.

4. Students independently write about an image of choice and their impression(s) derived from it.

Exploring key learnings through a compare and contrast model helps increase processing.

5. As a class, compare and contrast student thoughts and reactions with your lesson objective.

Visual ~ 9   Images: Conceiving a Quadrilateral

Student Concept Definition

Student Generated

When definitions are provided, learners may seek to memorize, even understand the meaning. When definitions or concepts are explored, and then derived from criteria, the essence of meaning emerges with enhanced understanding.

There are multiple approaches to this type of activity. You can present only items that "fit" into a category or definition; present items that do and don't fit... and make the distinction; or you can present items one at a time and let the students determine the criteria as you go. Consider the array of items below.

A graphic display of components that are contained in a group vs. those not in the group provides visual cues.

square	rectangle	**NOT** oval
NOT circle	rhombus	trapezoid
NOT triangle	**NOT** crossing lines	parallelogram

Some items are included. Some have **"NOT"** by them, indicating that they are not part of the set of items included in this grouping.

1.   Ask students to generate a list of characteristics that the items that are included all have in common. You may start with the square and ask, "What are the characteristics that you can identify that make up a square?" See list below.

2.   Then ask about the rectangle.

   ▪   "Which of the characteristics we've generated for a square also apply to a rectangle?"

   ▪   Note the **"NOT"** items in the second set - they do not apply to both shapes.

4 sides	parallel lines	four angles	4 equal sides
2 sets of parallel lines	4 lines	closed figure	4 right angles
L x W = Area			

Examining parts to generate a category.

4 sides	parallel lines	four angles	4 equal sides
2 sets of parallel lines	4 lines	closed figure	4 right angles
L x W = Area			

Compare / contrast is one of the most powerful approaches to sustain learning.

With each figure considered, fewer and fewer "criteria" match all of them.

4 sides	parallel lines	four angles	4 equal sides
2 sets of parallel lines	4 lines	closed figure	4 right angles
L x W = Area			

3. Tell students that the shapes included (vs. the **"NOT"** shapes) are called quadrilaterals. Ask them to look at the remaining characteristics and develop a definition of the term.

Social Learning System

4. Once they've considered this for a minute, have students work in small groups to develop their definition of a quadrilateral. Tell them they must develop the most concise definition possible that is also complete. For example:

   ▪ Some may say "a four sided figure." This is accurate, but not complete, as it does not mention that it must be a "closed" figure.

Concept development.

Exploring elements to form understanding of a whole.

5. When ready, have groups offer their definitions, seeing which one is the most concise, yet also complete in its elements of inclusion.

Visual ~ 10   Images: Differentiated Direction ~ Step Photo

Visual Sequences

Teacher or Student Generated

Manuals often have photographs to accompany written instructions. If students must follow a sequence, procedure or set of steps to accomplish a task, pictures can be "worth a thousand words," as the saying goes.

1. There are two approaches to this task:

Bimodal representations offer multiple pathways for understanding, memory, and recall.

Option A
- The teacher provides digital or Polaroid snapshots of each step of a process, procedure, sequence, or stage.

Option B
- Or the students - as part of their assignment, generate the photographs of each stage/step of the procedure.

Sequencing skills.

2. Assign students the task of following a set of directions, a procedure, whatever is part of your curriculum.

Half reference visual, half reference verbal.

3. Tell half of the class to use (or to create) the photographs for each step. Have the other half use the written instructions to follow the steps.

4. Ask the students to comment on the process. What was easy/helpful? What was difficult or hard to understand? What did they like/dislike about the reference material.

Aligning preferences with approach to a task.

5. As the teacher, ascertain which group has the most/least issues with the assignment. Try this with another group, but place the learners in preferred groups by asking them who would like to use photos vs. who would like to follow written directions. Again, ask questions about the process and see what students think.

Although some will do well with only one modality, most prefer, remember and recall better with both visual and verbal represented.

6. Try dividing the class into groups as follows:
- One group with written instructions, the other with both written and photographs.
- Another time, give one group photos only, the other group both.
- Ask them the same questions and see what works best.

Articulating at a meta-cognitive level helps learners understand how they learn.

7. Have students discuss the difference, how they felt, and how the process affected their thinking, learning and disposition toward the task.

Visual ~ 11 Images: Photo Facials and Interpersonal Cues

Visual Links to Emotional States Generate Lasting Memory

Visual imagery elicits feelings. Using images as a means to study human relations aligns with nonverbal cues. The importance of paying attention to posture and expression to ascertain another's disposition or mood is vital to interpersonal relations and toward making choices of interaction or approach.

Teacher Generated

1.   Select an image/photograph of a person with a distinct expression on their face:

   - Happy, sad, excited, afraid, etc.

2.   Show the image on a screen so that all students can see and examine it or provide each with a photo-copy of the face.

3.   Ask students to examine the photograph for about a minute to determine what they think the person is thinking or feeling - and write it down.

   - If capability permits.

4.   List student ideas on the board, noting similarities and differences in perceived thoughts and then of feelings.

Similar / Different

Social Learning System

   - Note the range of ideas in each category.
     - o   It is typical to have a broader range in "thinking" than in "feeling".

Expression/posture, Physical Learning System

   - Place students into pairs or triads to identify the specific things in the photograph that might have led them to perceive it as they did.
     - o   What are the cues that told you the person felt _____? (facial features)

Aligning preferences with approach to a task.

5.   Repeat this process with two more faces that represent different expressions than the first one. Experiment with different levels of subtlety as well as extremes.

Emotional Learning System

6.   Discuss how noticing subtle features on a person's face can help us to make decisions about what they are feeling and how we can best work with them.

Conflict management and interpersonal skills.

7.   Relate this to a current event or classroom circumstance, if appropriate, putting the observations into relevant context.

Visual ~ 12   Images: Photo Interest Groups

Visual Links to Ideas and Interests

Student Generated

Using visual image prompts as a means to select an item of interest can serve as a vehicle for learners to connect on an interest, prior to engaging in a task. Beginning a task that is interest-based or student-selected can help learners become and stay engaged.

1. Select an image/photograph that has a lot of detail in it. For example:

    - Foreground, background, detail, people, small and large objects, etc.

2. Show the image on a screen so that all students can see and examine it.

    - Option: You may use several images that have similar characteristics or copies of the same one to pass out so that each student can have his/her own to study.

Student selected focus

3. Ask students to examine the photograph for about a minute and then pick out one item in the photo that attracts them. Do not give them ideas regarding what might appeal to them. Let them select with as little input as possible.

4. Have students identify their selection (name it, highlight it, etc).

5. Ask the class to share the thing they selected. Record them on chart paper or the board.

Similarities and differences

6. Ask the class if some of the things people chose are either the same or similar by some characteristic (small vs. large objects, detail vs. major component, small, background vs. foreground, people vs. things, foods vs. animals vs. spices vs. plants and so forth). Form categories of items.

Social Learning System

7. Place students in groups by similarity of items selected.

Cognitive Learning System

8. Assign the small group a task that aligns with your objective, such as:

   - Brainstorm a list of words that describe your selections.

   - Identify the characteristics that you had in common among the items you selected.

   - Write a short story abut the role of your type of items in the photograph (small, background items play a supporting cast role, providing context for the main character or object in the image, or the animal in the photo suggests that the person enjoys creatures and portrays a personality based on the type of animal, or the main object/person is surrounded by contextual cues that help us understand who the person is or in what circumstance the object might fit).

   - OR, how would the photograph differ if your object were not in it?

   - OR, what item, added to the photograph, would change the main message?

Reflective Learning System

9. Have students comment on why they selected the type of item they did. For example:

   - Why a background item?

   - Why the main object?

   - Why a living thing?

   - etc.

Emotional Learning System

10. Ask students to describe the dominant feeling that the photograph portrays.

   - Why?

Visual ~ 13 Illustration: Referencing a Map

Creating Accompanying Visual References to Content

Aligning with dual coding theory, the mind stores information in "packets" that are comprised of both verbal and visual elements. Having students interact with visual representations relating to information to be learned enhances their capacity for understanding and recall.

Teacher Generated

Teacher selects a book to read. This may be a book read to the class or a book the class will read independently and work with during class time.

Some learners are more visually oriented than verbal. This assists their understanding of what the text is attempting to convey.

1. Tell the class that "we" or "they" (depending on the appropriateness to the objective and the capacity of learners) will be constructing "maps" of the journey the characters in the story will be taking.

Context is provided via the map, for students to get a sense or overview as they engage the content.

2. Assign (read) the first section (chapter). Provide students with a map of the journey. For example:

    ▪ Gulliver's Travels includes one in the book - or you will need to create one for students to use as the story progresses.

    ▪ At times, particularly if you are working with young children, you may want to create a class map together.

    ▪ Students can then copy this from the board or chart paper and have a personal copy to work with.

3. After having read the section, ask students to review the map and "track" the journey with a pencil (permanent markers can be used at an appropriate time).

Physical Learning System is engaged and integrated with visual.

A quick "glance" at a visual can often provide key information to a teacher about what a student is thinking. It can also provide feedback to the student in a timely manner.

- Repeat this process of linking the visual map with sections of the reading intermittently.

- At times it may be sufficient to have students work independently. At other times, you may want to have students work in small groups to discuss each other's map and to compare ways to depict the story's progress.

- Also, it would be helpful to periodically discuss or review the map(s) as a class, as a way of providing feedback to everyone or to get an idea of how each child is doing.

Visual ~ 14   Illustration: Map Memory

Creating Explicit Visuals to Accompany Content

Student Generated

Aligning with dual coding theory, the mind stores information in "packets" that are comprised of both verbal and visual elements. Having students create and interact with visual representations of information to be learned enhances their capacity for understanding and recall.

Teacher selects a book to read. This may be a book read to the class (commonly PK-3) or a book the class will read independently and discuss or interpret during class time.

Dual Coding: Some learners are more visual oriented than verbal. This assists their understanding of what the text is attempting to convey.

Working in groups engages the Social Learning System.

1. Tell the class that they will be generating "maps" to portray the journey the characters in the story will be taking, or to capture a setting or circumstance.

    ▪ You may want each student to have their own map, so that activities outside of school time can be conducted.

    ▪ Another approach would be to have sub-groups generate a group map (in which discussions about entries would take place as a group).

Context is provided via a map helps students gain a sense of how things relate to one another, which provides meaning to events or actions.

2. Assign (read) the first section (chapter).

    ▪ Ask students to generate a map of the journey the characters are taking, or have them construct a map of "Main St." (or the city, town or country in which the story takes place).

    ▪ Students could also create a map of a country being studied. They can locate the buildings, side roads, and/or geography and the proximity of one place to another.

    ▪ At times, particularly if you are working with young children, you may want to create this map together as a class--or at least a version that each student or group can reference.

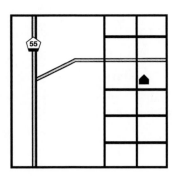

3. After having read designated sections of the material, ask students to review their map and log the journey, or to enter pertinent elements (swamp, mountains, city hall, etc.).

Physical Learning System is engaged and integrated with visual.

A quick "glance" at a visual can often provide key information to a teacher about what a student is thinking. It can also provide feedback to the student in a timely manner.

Working in groups engages the Social Learning System.

Timely feedback is important to secure learning. Conceptual and relational aspects of curriculum in visual representations provide key reference cues for both teachers and students along the way.

▪ Repeat the process of discussing and checking the visual map with sections of the reading/material intermittently.

▪ At times you may want to have students work in small groups to discuss each other's map and to compare ways to depict the story's progress. They can help each other understand various perspectives and to include important items.

▪ This can serve as a vehicle for formative feedback that helps learners stay on course and avert misconceptions.

▪ In the end, visual representations inform us about how a learner sees things, their relationship to one another and their importance to big ideas and essential concepts. They are wonderful inputs for summative assessments as well.

Reflective Learning System

4. Assign homework at some point that requires students to involve a family member. For example:

▪ Have them ask a parent to look at the map and make a prediction about what they think will happen next.

Visual ~ 15   Illustration: Mapping the Final Exam

Clarifying Assessment Targets and Impediments

Student Generated

Aligning with dual coding theory, the mind stores information in "packets" that are comprised of both verbal and visual elements. Having students identify words and phrases that are not known prior to a unit of study can help the teacher address vocabulary and meaning of important terms in explicit ways. This will help assure greater student success.

Teacher gives a copy of the final exam or assessment questions, problems, or an alternative form of the assessment to the students on the first day of the new chapter or unit of study.

The early identification of potential difficulties can help set learning goals.

1. Ask the students to review the assessment and identify any terms, phrases or other items they are not familiar with or do not know.

Take care that the assessment is measuring the intended content, concept or information - and that vocabulary and other issues are not interfering with the outcome.

2. Make a list of all items identified by students.

- Some items are the content/concepts to be addressed in the unit.
- Other items may be specific terms, new vocabulary or other items that will inhibit student understanding and success if not addressed.
- Post this list in a place visible to all students.

Linking visual cues early on can help increase understanding and reduce unnecessary blocks to learning.

3. Take time before beginning the new chapter or unit and review each appropriate item.

- Take care not to define terms or ideas, but to "depict" them with images, characteristics, contexts, and/or graphics. For example: maps, diagrams, etc.

A quick "glance" at a visual can often provide key information to a student that provides retrieval cues that can keep the student on track--on task.

4. Generate "posters" and/or other visuals for the students to reference as their work progresses.

- Hang the posters on the class walls during the unit of study.

Co-constructing visuals to accompany the verbal/cognitive elements of learning enhances all learner's abilities for retention and recall.

5. Add to the posters and graphics as the work continues. Ultimately, have students add words, meanings, and eventually definitions.

"Mid-course" feedback is essential to mid-course corrections that promote greater success on final or summative assessments.

6. Provide a mid-unit, mid-chapter assessment to see how students are doing with the key ideas and vocabulary. This is a low-stakes opportunity for feedback - not a graded assessment.

- In the end, the assessment should not be on vocabulary, but rather on the main ideas of the unit.

Visual ~ 16   Illustration: Generating Vocabulary "Picts"

Building Vocabulary with Representations

Teacher Generated

Creating bimodal packets associated with unknown words or ideas helps the learner establish contextual meaning.

First, determine and create the assessment(s) you will use for a unit or chapter or body of work.

Learning need not be a mystery. Students should be aware of what they will be studying and what the expected results are.

If there is vocabulary that may prohibit optimal learning of the curriculum, then identify it early and address it explicitly.

1. Prior to instruction, review the materials and identify any words or phrases students are likely to be unfamiliar with or uncertain about - words that may potentially interfere with their understanding.

Option to have students work together in small groups to generate vocabulary "picts."

2. List the identified words on chart paper. Ask students to select one to three words each to work with for today.

    ▪   You can continue this process each day until all words have been covered - or assign words to groups of students for initial review.

Use of illustration to construct relationships between ideas.

3. Provide students with an image, photo or picture for each word. Have each student or group identify descriptors that they feel apply to the word or phrase selected.

Building meaning and context are more powerful strategies toward vocabulary development than defining terms.

4. Ask students to create posters of each word or phrase, complete with the image provided by the teacher. Instruct them that they need to arrange space on the poster to accommodate several descriptors (words/phrases), as well as additional images or drawings they decide upon.

5. As students begin, present brief explanations and descriptions of each word/phrase they will encounter... but **refrain from either providing or looking up definitions** !!!

Having learners generate their own understanding, rather than memorizing a definition, will create more memory and recall.

6. Have students create their poster for each word/phrase. At first, pencil may be wise - in case they decide later on to alter any part of the poster.

Early visual, repeated referencing of meanings will enhance the acquisition of new terms.

7. Hang posters where all can reference them as needed. Periodically, ask students to review the posters to update, alter, or add information to them - as well as to insure their accuracy.

Reflection helps strengthen learning pathways.

8. Take time to re-do the posters if, and as, needed.

Visual ~ 17   Illustration: The Illustration/Analogy Intersection

Transferring Concepts

Teacher Generated

The transfer of ideas from one subject or area of understanding to another can serve to embed learning and enhance recall.

Learning numerous pieces of data.

Use of illustration to link a learning skill with usage.

Generate a graphic representation that is analogous to the skill being taught. For example:

- English/Language Arts; Mechanics; Using capitals and periods in daily writing.

Teachers have the option to develop this illustration analogy as a team and present it to the class, or to ask the class for input/ideas as the illustration is generated.

1.   Using the example provided, the teachers ask themselves (or the class) what familiar things or activities have similarities to the mechanics of capitals and periods.

- Brainstorming might include green light/red light; begin/end; start/stop; front/back; first/last; etc.

2.   Generate a metaphoric illustration that is commonly recognized and depicts the mechanics of capital and period. It must be easily understood and link clearly with the learning objective. For example:

- A car has bumpers at each end - that represent front/back; begin/end; first/last.

- Draw a car, emphasizing the bumpers, coloring them red and green. Green represents "go" or the starting place - which is aligned with using a capital to begin a sentence.

Setting up a unit of study with concept development prior to content exploration.

- Red represents "stop" or the ending place - which is aligned with using a period.

The fast taxi was ready for its next passengers.

3. Place the illustration (large enough to be viewable from all areas of the room) up for all to reference.

Referencing the metaphor during use or analogy.

4. Remind students as they begin an assignment to "use bumpers on each sentence."

5. Just before collecting student work, remind them again to "check their bumpers" before handing in their work.

Visual ~ 18   Illustration: Concept Illustration

Illustrating Concepts and Big Ideas

Student Generated

Aligning with dual coding theory, the mind stores information in "packets" that are comprised of both verbal and visual elements. Having students create and interact with visual representations of concepts enhances their capacity for the transfer and application of big ideas.

Working in groups engages the Social Learning System.

1. Place students in groups of 3-5. Provide paper (11x17 or larger) and writing/drawing implements. For example: markers, crayons, etc.

Concepts provide an arena, a context for other information to increase in meaning, value or purpose. They are vehicles for transfer and application.

2. The teacher selects a key concept central to the unit of study (democracy, photosynthesis, geography, loyalty, etc.) and presents it to the class by writing it on the board/chart paper. For example:

   - This activity will use "democracy."

Visualizing creates networks that can link ideas.

Exploring options prior to engaging in production creates opportunity for divergent activity prior to converging on producing outputs.

3. **Without talking or writing anything,** students are asked to take one minute and visualize the term or idea... to consider what images or thoughts come to mind.

   - "What comes to mind when you think of democracy?"
   - They need to do this in silence, prior to engaging in discussion or attempting to produce outcomes.

Social Learning System

4. Now ask students to discuss their ideas with each other in their small groups. Once reviewed, they can determine how they wish to capture their thoughts and images on the paper provided. Some groups will decide on a theme and construct a unified image with related sub-components. Other groups may decide to have each member contribute their own component or idea, generating a variety of "pieces" of the overall conceptual puzzle.

   - This aspect can take anywhere from a few minutes to a half hour. More time could be justified based on the lesson objective. Most often, it is not necessary.

A quick "glance" at a visual can often provide key information to a teacher about what students are thinking. It can also provide an array of ideas for consideration by others.

Conceptual and relational aspects of curriculum in visual representations provide key reference cues for both teachers and students.

5. Have groups post their illustrations around the room when they have completed them. Ask the class to do a "walk around" and observe how each group constructed their visual, and which components they chose to depict the concept.

6. As students return to their seats, ask each group to briefly explain their illustration and what they were intending to capture. Note with the class the variety of ways students depicted the same concept.

    ▪   In this example, the illustrations provide access to prior knowledge and concept representations of all learners for the class to consider, prior to engaging in new material/the unit.

Reflective Learning System

7. Assign homework at some point that requires students to involve a family member. For example:

    ▪   Have them ask a parent what the concept means to them and have them suggest an image that comes to mind, along with 3-4 key words they think of in respect to the concept.

Visual ~ 19   Illustration: Unit Illustration

Representing Understanding Through Illustration

Student Generated

Having students create visual representations of concepts as they relate to sub-components generates a perspective of relationships between elements that enhances capacity for understanding ideas.

1. Students work individually for this activity. Provide each student with two sheets of paper (11x17 or larger).

Orientations to upcoming studies can help provide context for learners in developing their skills and understandings.

2. Provide an overview of the unit. For example:

   - Climate: briefly (five minutes) provide an orientation to the content and ideas to be explored. Write key vocabulary terms on the board and discuss them with the class as a general review of their meanings.

Illustrating subordinate ideas and details as they relate to big ideas helps to organize thinking and understanding... giving meaning to relationships.

By making two copies, it will be easy to make pre-post comparisons as portrayed in the ongoing, updated representation of learning (as lessons progress).

This provides visual feedback that teachers, students, and parents can readily understand.

3. Assure students that they are not expected to fully understand the topic at the beginning of a unit. Ask students to create a mind map that illustrates their thinking around a topic/unit of study they will begin. When completed to the best of their ability, have them replicate it on the second sheet of paper. See the example for "climate" below.

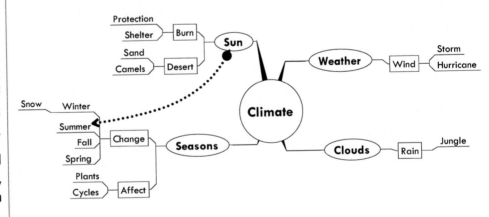

- As you teach each lesson of the unit, provide a few minutes each time for students to take out their "illustration" of climate and add/change/alter components.

Bimodal visual/verbal linkages.	

- **Changes** — At various point, students will need a fresh piece of paper to reconstruct ideas, relationships between components, placement on the paper, etc.

- **Alternative Connectors** — Some may even use string or yarn to connect things, so they can change them without having to recreate the entire drawing.

- **Structural Options** — Some may want to support the paper with cardboard (or some other rigid material) underneath, so they can glue or attach items that are three-dimensional.

- **Writing** — You may request that students write short paragraphs on index cards to explain a few key components - that would not otherwise fit on the growing illustration.

Identifying personal learning. When students can "see" that they have learned and note the positive difference between their prior knowledge and their new level of understanding - it is motivational!

4. Have groups display their illustrations around the room when they have completed them. Place the original version (the second copy you have saved from the first day's work) beside the final illustration.

5. Ask students to walk about the room and notice key differences between the first and final illustrations. It should be clear, even from a short glance, that the understandings of concepts and information has shifted - and grown immensely.

Inviting parents to successfully participate or acknowledge their child's work/learning.

- The culminating activity of displaying the pre-and post illustrations makes for a wonderful parent's night or open house experience. Parents can easily see the difference between the two portrayals, and be pleased with the progress their son/daughter has made.

Reflective Learning System

6. Assign homework at some point that requires students to ask a family member to offer two ideas/concepts/terms for the student to add to their illustration.

Visual ~ 20 Illustration: Interest Wall Graphics

Personalizing Interests and Linking Words

Creating a visual for all students that captures their interests and builds vocabulary. Having visual cues available as a reference helps to both establish memory, and to provide retrieval cues.

Student & Teacher Generated

Generating interest from familiarity and outside activities.

1. Ask each student what s/he is interested in. For example:
   - Hobby, area of interest, activity, etc.

Linking interest and visual media.

2. Have each student locate a picture (or draw one) that corresponds with their interest area. For example:
   - Old magazines, newspaper, website, etc.

Linking verbal and visual.

3. Place these pictures on a wall (bulletin board), clustered around "Our Interests." Have students write a word or phrase to describe their image.

The cluster to the right shows circles--that would be both the image and the word entries. Creating a pictorial view that provides context for all to see relationships between individual items as well as to have a personal link to the work.

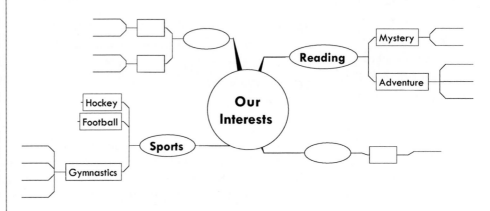

Linking similar interests.

- If some student interests are similar (reading) then ask if they have preferences (adventure, mystery) and create sub-categories of that interest area (see graphic above).

Building on interest and prior knowledge.

4. Periodically, have students add a related image and/or word to their interest entry in the cluster.

5. Have students build a vocabulary of terms around their image/area.

Illustration of building vocabulary related to a single category.

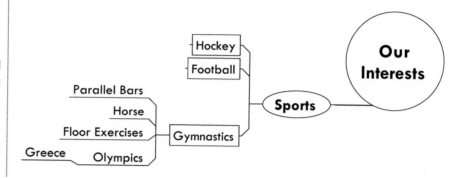

Using prior knowledge and interest to invite learners to participate through an area of strength.

6. Reference the interests periodically in class discussions, asking students to provide an example related to their interest area. Also, the interests may be useful as prompts for student reports, writing stories, and homework related assignments.

Visual ~ 21   Illustration: Create an Advertisement

Conveying Meaning Visually

Student choice is a vehicle to engagement. Creating illustrations from personal interest and meaning is a powerful tool for generating and connecting ideas.

Student Generated

This exercise can be applied to persuasive writing, building an argument or supporting detail for a main idea - among other options.

Student interest provides meaning. Allowing choice increases motivation.

1.   The objective is for students to construct an advertisement that promotes a topic/item of their choice.

- Let students select the topic/content of their promotion.
- Assign the task to students, to promote their idea, policy, method or product.

Establishing the criteria or goals ahead of time helps learners understand the elements required for successful performance.

2.   Work with students to develop criteria for effective advertising or persuasiveness. This will be the criterion the class will use to assess each advertisement when they have been completed.

- Be sure to post the criteria for all to see while working on this project.

Use of illustration to construct relationships between ideas.

3.   Ask students to construct reasons why their selected item/topic/etc. should be of interest to prospective buyers. Have them determine effective ways to promote the use or sale of their idea/topic.

- Encourage them to use illustrations, graphics, and/or pictures to connect with their audiences.

4.   Have students post their advertisements.

Applying criteria for successful performance helps to embed the use of important learnings.

5.   Invite the class to walk around the room and view the ads. Give each a set of criteria to use to assess each piece.

- Ask students questions about why any given ad impressed them on each of the criteria.

Visual ~ 22 Illustration: Algorithm Balloons

Learning Math Formulas Through Visual References

Student & Teacher Generated

When the mind makes images, it develops conceptual understanding. Unknowns are common in our lives. Capturing illustrations of terms and abstractions helps to depict meaning.

1. Write on the board an algorithm, or a common formula you will be using in the upcoming unit or chapter.

2. Have students copy this algorithm on an 8 1/2 x 11 piece of paper, leaving room above the mathematical sentence. See below.

Students do the work of learning.

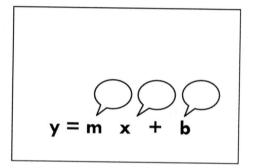

3. Discuss each letter and its meaning with the class.

    ▪ On the board, above each of the letters to the right of the "equals" sign, draw in a cartoon bubble.

Visual references for abstract elements.

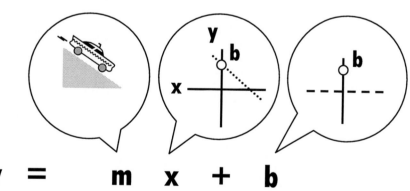

Discussing the meaning of abstract symbols that are unknown to learners can help them gain understanding. Working together to generate illustrations of each "unknowns" helps to secure this understanding in memory.

4. As you discuss the meaning of each "unknown," have students indicate what images form in their minds. For example:

- The "m" = slope.

- Therefore, have students draw representations of "slope" in the bubble above "m."

- Some will draw a car moving down a ramp - the ramp being the slope.

- Do the same for both "x" and "b," however, have them do "m" and "b" before tackling "x."

Cognitive Learning System

Visual cues to personal meaning.

It is not only text that benefits from bimodal memory cues. Math sentences also are greatly enhanced with visual references.

- In our illustration, "x" is represented as a see-saw board, depicting that there is a direct relationship between "y" and "x" values.

- This is not to mean that there are not other ways to capture this - or that this is necessarily accurate in all cases. It is a place to begin the visual side of understanding the function of "x."

- The "b" is represented as the place where the vertical axis line is intersected. Again, variations exist.

- The options from here are many and as varied as you make them, for applications and examples from applied learning references. The object of this exercise is to help students form imagery that provides a basis for initial understanding.

Visual ~ 23   Illustration: The Reflection Pool: What Qualities Do You Want to See?

Art, Visual Concepts, and Personal Reflection

This exercise is the brainchild of John Norton. John is a practicing artist as well as a veteran educator at Buckingham, Browne, and Nichols School in Cambridge, MA.

Student Generated

- Although this project can be done with beginning art students, it works better as experience is amassed.

- Each student has to be honest and fairly introspective for this to work to its full potential.

- The experience has potential for exposing a deeper level about who students are and how they feel. Therefore, it may be wise to use this approach only with students who have established supportive relationships with each other.

- The potential lies within for a group experience that can be powerfully transforming.

Reflective Learning System

Personalizing the assignment.

1. Toward the mid-year, ask students to identify a personal quality that they do not feel they have yet but would like to possess. This is not an object or something that you can physically possess (good looks, money, athletic grace, etc) but a virtuous inner quality that can only be expressed abstractly.

- John Norton typically does this activity with 2nd year drawing or painting students.

- John Norton asks the students to associate a name with the quality for clarity's sake. For example:
  - Patience, humility, courage, spontaneity, trust, perseverance, generosity, etc.

Bimodal packets employed to link visual aspects of thought and memory with verbal elements.

2. Ask students to create a visual expression of the quality they selected. They may express this any way they want - in any size, varied materials, 2D or 3D, so long as it does not refer to anything other than itself. This is crucial. It must be totally abstract or "non-objective" in terms of art. Warn against using easy symbols or clichéd images that are familiar. For example:

- If it is "freedom" that a student desires, how would s/he express "desire?" What would represent freedom to him/her?

- Suggest that students take time to "root around" awhile to get to the essence of the gift that they are giving themselves.

- Urge students to pick their materials very carefully. The results are usually varied and unpredictable.

3. Insist that they tell no one what their piece of art represents, to sneak it in secretly to class on the due date, and to be prepared to talk about how they made it.

Attending to visual cues.

4. During the review, ask all students in the class to try to identify the qualities that are embedded in each work. Afterwards, have them try to identify who did which piece.

Student assessment of their work and the work in general provides feedback regarding adjustments to the learning assignment as well as to future work on other tasks.

5. Lastly, talk about whether the exercise was interesting or not, and why.

- Most of John Norton's students say the experience was quite interesting., Many say it was the best, or perhaps the most personal thing they had ever done in art.

- Remind the students that when art succeeds, it works on a deeply personal and symbolic level.

- Be sure to thank them for being willing to try this way of making art.

Closing comments from John Norton:

- "The "self-portrait" is an old, time-tested assignment in high school art curriculum. The variation above is a nontraditional self-portrait. Oddly enough, the more abstract the self-portrait, the freer the student response. Many times students do not risk enough with their art and miss out on expanding their consciousness because of it."

A historical perspective with rationale for many aspects of this assignment.

- "The idea for doing this project came to me about 15 years ago when I realized that, although I was teaching the technical skills needed to draw and paint, what I really was after is that students learn to trust their own creative process more. This meant focusing on themselves more and specifically learning to overcome their fear of failure or rejection in art. Much of that fear comes from two sources: either they think that they cannot express what they want (they lack the skills to make "good art") or they worry that what they create will be too personal and therefore unacceptable to others (their art is too "weird.") How would I address those issues somehow?"

- "Oddly enough, one path led directly to abstract art and its possibilities to express personal states of mind. I also know, from first hand experience, that one of the keys to making art is to see shapes, forms, and abstract visual relationships as having meaning in and of themselves. Also, it's important to challenge our left brain's tendency to label the visual world and thereby be blinded to its visual connections, as Betty Edwards pointed out so well in her first book. Johannes Itten and the Bauhaus teachers in Germany had taken art education in a new direction when they pioneered the study of how emotion and abstract art are interrelated. The post WWII Abstract Expressionist painters of New York understood and believed in this. Betty Edwards and art therapists seem to understand this as well. The problem is that young learners think that mucking around in art is just nonsense, anyone can do it, anyone can be a Pollock. But, then things change when you get them to look at one square inch of a painting and get them to see how inherently abstract vision really is.) If you make a series of random gestures or lines on a piece of paper, 95% of the students will agree that it is a thing, a person or creature, or a spatial landscape of sorts. Youth want to read content into abstraction and this is useful to me as a teacher because if they can do that it helps them open up to the whole range of possibilities in seeing how the visual world is inherently abstract. I tell them the Oliver Sach's story about the adult man recently sighted who could not make sense out of the visual world."

- "Finally, this exercise helps me introduce the idea of style: it gives the kids free license to explore new ways of expressing their feelings and ideas with an approach that is their own. This feeds into the ongoing debate in the adolescent's brain - over the idea of art's worthiness and whether or not it is attached to art's recognizability. Students are obsessed with what makes something "real." Is objectively-based art more "real' than abstract art? What happens if students are forced to confront the fact that abstract art can be a valid way to express profoundly real personal qualities or states of mind precisely because it does not refer to specific objects? It only refers to itself and therein lies its usefulness. Once students grasp this idea they relax some, start to redefine what makes art good' or ""bad"" and begin to let personal ideas "emerge in their work."

John Norton can be reached at john_norton@bbns.org.

Sensory ~ 24 Oral Exchanges: Role Reversal

Trying on a New Mind Set

Student Generated

When the student becomes the teacher (in a teacher role), his or her psychological status is elevated. During such a time, the attentional system is more fully engaged and a likelihood of increased processing occurs.

Learning numerous pieces of data

When learning a substantial set of items that have links, such as states and capitals, the "location" in spatial context can provide a nonlinguistic cue that helps memory.

Use of illustration to link a learning skill with usage

1. Provide students with a map of the United States with state borders. Students can trace and create their own maps if desired.

2. Have students select a state of their choice and color/ shade it in.

3. On the back of the map paper, have students write the name of the state and its capitol. An example is provided below.

State Name	*Maine*	State Capital	*Augusta*
correct	III	correct	II
incorrect		incorrect	I

Other Information
1.
2.
3.

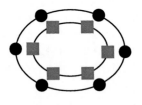

4. Divide the class in half. Instruct half of the class to form a circle and face outward.

5. Ask the other half of the class to form a circle around the first group, facing inward. Each person should be facing a classmate.

Linking a spatial context of "shape" with cognitive information to form a memory cue or link

6. Students in the inside circle show their drawings (map of the US with a shaded state) to their partner, asking them to name the state that has been shaded/colored and its capital.

Student as teacher	7. As students respond and answer with a state and capital, the student holding the paper records the response as correct or incorrect, with a tally mark on the back of the paper. Instruct the students to inform their partner whether their answer was correct or not. If not, tell them what the correct response was.
Social Learning System	8. After the inside circle students have "quizzed" their partners, the outside circle students reciprocate and "quiz" the inside circle using their sheet, recording responses as well.
Teaching new information	9. When both partners (inside and outside circles) have finished, they swap sheets, each taking the other person's state. They now have the other person's state to quiz someone else on.

10. When all are done with this round (round #1), tell the outside circle students to remain still while the inside circle students move 3 people to their right (they need to move far enough so that their new partner could not overhear the prior exchange.

11. Have the new partners repeat the process.
   - Again, have partners exchange papers/states and have the inside circle move three people to the right.
   - Repeat this process only three or four times.

12. Ask students to return to their seats.

Timely feedback for correction or to be addressed can create more accurate learning and avert significant "unlearning" needs	13. When done, either ask the class to offer information about what states and capitols were missed, or collect the sheets and tabulate the correct/incorrect marks yourself. This provides feedback about which states and capitals may need further review.

Sensory ~ 25 *Math "Line-Up" Teams*

Alternative Approaches to Learning

Teacher Generated

Having students contribute to a team effort can enhance motivation. Shifting emphasis from oral to silent creates a unique experience that increases the attentional system. Explicit discussion of performance strategies helps students understand alternative approaches to learning.

1. Form teams of four or with equal numbers.

Social Learning System

- One piece of paper is placed on a table with the answer/response written at the top.
  - For example: " = 4 " for each team.
- One pencil is used for each team.

Reducing or eliminating verbal exchanges (talking) causes learners to rely on other processing patterns to determine how to participate

2. Each team member enters one item and then goes to the back of the line. There is no talking during this exercise.

- Members must stay in order and only one entry at a time.
  - For example: " 5 − 1. "
- Entry must differ from any others already written.
  - For example: " 6 − 2, " " 8 − 4, " "-3 + 7, " etc.
- Silence: members may not "tell" the person writing what to write.

3. When time is up, have a member from another team visit to tabulate the number of different, correct responses.

4. Determine which team was able to achieve the most correct responses in the time available.

Conceptualizing how to accomplish a task, as well as how to work together makes learning explicit

5. Have teams discuss the strategies they used or discovered, then have them share with the class.

First attempts enable learning and understanding. Offering a "second try" allows learners to "learn" from their early efforts.

6. Conduct another trial and repeat process.

7. The number of correct items by all teams should improve by using patterns that are more efficient.

- For example: " 0 + 4 ", " 1 + 3 ", " 2 + 2 ", " 3 + 1 ", " 4 + 0."

Sensory ~ 26 Story Fold Cells

Physical Models in Steps

Creating a physical model that represents the steps of a procedure or process helps to identify each segment and create visually tagged inputs and cues.

Teacher Generated

Learning a process or sequence of steps

1. Hand out paper and ask students to fold it over three times. This will create 8 boxes when unfolded. In this scenario, the students will only be using 6 out of the 8 boxes.

2. Have the students number the first six boxes as shown.

1
2
3
4
5
6

Use of illustration to link a learning skill with usage

3. Provide the word problem for students to work out. For example:

    Jules went to the beach to collect seashells. When he returned, he counted a total of 15 shells. Sorting by size, he put 3 big shells in a container with a red lid. He put 6 medium shells in a container with a green lid. How many small shells did Jules have left to put in the container with a red lid?

Model of the problem in steps. Either the teacher can model or request that the students develop their own model.

4. Have students place manipulatives or draw the following:
    - 15 items (shells) in the first box.
    - 3 large items (shells) in the second box.
    - 6 medium items (shells) in the third box.
    - 3 large and 6 medium items (shells) in the fourth box (addition).
    - 15 items (shells) in the fifth box:
        ○ draw a line through 3 large items (shells).
        ○ draw another line through 6 medium items (shells).
        ○ now they can solve for the sum of the large and medium shells.
    - The remaining items (shells) is the solution.

5.   Ask students to use this process of constructing their own images or representations for two more problems using folded paper. Check to see their work before they "discard" manipulatives from the paper.

6.   Option: Have the students write the words, "addition, subtraction, and solution: in the appropriate boxes.

Or, have them write them on paper and cut these out so they can be placed on the boxes in the paper. This way they can be reused over and over.

Sensory ~ 27 Moving Continuums ~ Committing with Body in Space

Seeing Predictions Come to Life

Teacher Generated

When someone must commit to a prediction or position regarding a topic or solution, and additional sensory systems are engaged, the process can result in enhanced memory being embedded with longer range and better recall.

Making predictions or hypotheses

1. Place words or phrases on a wall that establish a continuum for the topic of discussion. For instance, you could put "no control" at one end of the wall and "full or complete control" at the other end.

   - The possibilities are endless, but should relate to your lesson objective.

   - Other dichotomies might be from costly to free, easy to hard, or like to dislike.

   - Another way to create a continuum would be with a gradation of number value, such as "Rate how you feel about whether neighbors should interfere with problems taking place in other people's homes, from 1 = should not to 10 = absolutely should."

Think independently prior to collectively

2. Ask the students to consider a question, like "How much influence do you have regarding policies and practices at this school?"

Taking a stand or committing caused more excitatory activity in the brain

3. After a minute, ask the students to leave their seats and go stand along the wall in a place that represents their view. Tell them they can select a place at any point in between the two ends that portrays any level of influence they feel they might have.

4. While the students are still standing, discuss the number of people at each location. It is important to focus on how "many" have similar beliefs or views on the topic, rather than "who."

5. Ask the students to take their seats. Continue the discussion of the pros and cons and various ways students are removed, restricted in their involvement, or could be invited into the process of influencing policy or practices at the school.

   - Generate a list of ideas.

Transferring ideas into organized thought and writing	6. Now ask the students to look at the possibilities raised by the discussion, and have them write a short essay or position paper on the topic.
Revisit hypothesis or earlier perspective	7. After the writing is well underway, invite students to view the continuum on the wall one more time. Ask them to recall where they had placed themselves earlier and where they would go to now, after the discussion and paper they had written.
Recommit	8. Have students return to the wall at the SAME PLACE they had first gone. Once all are standing, ask them to move (if needed) to where they now "stand" on the issue. Take note of who moves.
	9. Separate the class into two groups: those who did not move to a new position and those who did move.
Identifying pertinent elements underling ideas and perspectives	10. Ask each group to discuss why the points made, pro or con, did or did not influence their decision to move. Discuss their impressions. • Some beliefs are difficult to change. • Can the class identify any categories of reasons? For example: cultural, long history involving this issue, cynicism, etc.
Applying learning to relevant situations	11. Now ask the students to write a short paper on how they would approach an issue that is of interest to them. Encourage them to write the paper as if they were to address it in hopes of initiating changes.

Sensory ~ 28 Interdisciplinary & Sensory Parallels

Explaining the Big Idea and Creating a Framework for Learning

Creating a physical model with analogous representations of a concept across disciplines and senses.

Student Generated

Identifying the underlying big idea/s

The teacher identifies the big idea, essential question, or overarching (underlying) concept that the unit will address.

Starting with a concept is important, as it provides a context in which they can determine purpose or meaning of ensuing information.

1. Explain the big idea (concept to be explored) to students to insure all have a general grasp of overall meaning. Discuss this for overall meaning and application as follows below (this assumes that the general concept is readily acknowledged by learners, such as in the example provided. If not, then another approach may be required).

Explanation and Illustration

Below is an illustration of an approach to a unit of study. The divided circle on the right represents a set of lessons which, when completed, will comprise the unit of study. Each triangle in the middle represents a lesson. We provide several lessons, each building toward a desired body of knowledge or set of skills. On the left, is the concept. We know what this is prior to beginning instruction - however, the learners may not. Providing the concept first gives learners a context in which to place information while they search for meaning or purpose.

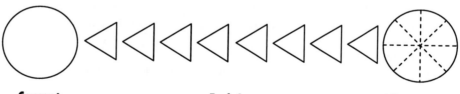

Concept   **Each Lesson**   **All Lessons**

This example will review the beginning of a chapter/unit of study on parallel lines. Students of most ages understand the notion of parallel. A simple visual gesture, moving both hands a few inches apart simultaneously across the air, cues learners about the gist of the concept.

▪   **Allow for at least two responses to each area of discipline.**

Power of second wait time: Pausing after the first student response (and not commenting) invites additional recall and more thought--increasing the amount of student processing.	**2.** Ask the class to answer a question across multiple disciplines:

2. Ask the class to answer a question across multiple disciplines:

- Science: "Where in nature - living,, growing things - do you see examples of parallels?" (cornstalks, grass, the legs of a cow, etc).
  - ○ Wait for at least two responses before moving on.

- Geography: "Where in geography - land, water, rock formations-- do you see evidence of parallels?" For example: sedimentary layers, cleavage in crystals, river banks, etc.
  - ○ Wait for at least two responses before moving on.

Having students generate examples from their experiences and perceptions embeds new learning more than teacher provided examples.

- Fine arts: "Where in the fine arts - music, drawing, painting, photography - do you see parallels?" For example: music staff lines, picture frame sides, or strings on an instrument.
  - ○ Wait for at least two responses before moving on.

- Do three or four disciplines only. Continuing across more could be a reasonable homework assignment, but the point has been made after a few examples - that parallels are everywhere.

Paradoxical Intentions create dissonance in the mind. This strategy can cause increased processing in the mind--as a means to determining the origin or resolve of a discord--and result in more mental networking or recall.

3. Paradox: Now ask students to "reverse" the process, by asking them, "Where in the world of athletics and sporting events, can you find an activity that DOES NOT have parallels associated with it?"

- By asking for EXclusions rather than INclusions, the mind must search now for where circumstances exist that do not have the concept under consideration. This stimulates very active processing, causing each learner to review familiar sporting events, only to find parallels associated with them. For example: football = gridlines, baseball = opposing base paths, etc.

See the book, "Creating Mindsets..." by R.K. Greenleaf for additional information.

Pulling information from mental "pictures" helps to access recall.

4. At some point, someone will venture a response. Ask the class if they can find an example of parallel in that area. Most likely, they will. It's not about "right/wrong," but rather, about how the mind revisits known and conjectured memories and actively searches for things - in this case, parallels.

- By searching for where something is NOT, we discover how prevalent it is.

Having learners tap into existing mental imagery forms a context that helps keep new information available while new ideas are being explored.

5. Have learners identify a hobby or favorite music CD. Assign homework or class time for them to find an example of "parallel" in or on the hobby/CD. They can share this verbally in class or depict it on paper as an illustration of the concept of parallel.

Personalizing a concept to student meaning will help strengthen memory and recall.

- The capacity for the learner to add new information, to build on an existing concept, is improved. With greater understanding of a concept, the context generated serves to provide a "place" where new information is more likely to be stored while we continue to construct new ideas, categories and understandings.

Having learners access information already in their repertoire, they can more easily keep new ideas "available" in attempts to create links, connect with existing information and build new understandings.

Emotional Learning System engaged to assist, not block

Comprehension regarding existing familiarity with a concept, prior to exploring new levels of understanding and application, allows for a more positive disposition toward acquiring additional information or skills - as the resistance or emotional fears are lessened, and the belief in probable success is increased.

This exercise causes learners to review prior knowledge, mentally searching for images of known experiences and information to respond to the query. When the student does the "work," the processing necessary for learning to be generated, and the opportunities for sustained memory are increased.

6. Now ask students to use their senses to explore the concept. Examples might be:

Integrating senses with the concept to be learned.

- **Hearing** Similar sounds like a bird chirping and a chipmunk squeaking, waves on the ocean and wind in trees, or tire noise on the highway.

Student experiences of personal meaning from memory.

- **Seeing** Lines in a book are written in parallel, two geese flying along side each other, or side-by-side tracks in snow or on the beach.

Physical Learning System a la the senses.

- **Touching** The feel of an ant crawling on your foot, a blade of grass touching your ankle, touching sandpaper, or touching a cinder block.

Reflective Learning System.

- **Smelling** Campfire odors and mother's cooking, perfume and a favorite aunt, match smoke and candles.

- **Tasting** A new recipe and a favorite food, the crunch of peanuts and chow mien noodles, lobster and crab.

Sensory ~ 29   Interdisciplinary & Sensory Perceptions

Perceiving Through the Senses

Inquiring about multiple representations across sensory perceptions immerses learners in perspectives that stimulate varied sensory channels.

Student Generated

In a chapter/unit/storybook or other appropriate area of study, have students stop and consider how to describe or depict a character, a historical figure, a circumstance or situation, etc.

1.   Ask learners to describe or depict what the person is wearing, carrying or what the essential elements of the circumstance or era in time may be.

2.   List the descriptors on the board.

Metacognition via a sensory area will focus learners on how any given sense may bear on the situation or alter one's perspective.

3.   Divide the class into 4-5 groups. Assign each group a sense: seeing, hearing, tasting, touching, smelling, and perhaps even feeling.

4.   Ask each group to explore 3-5 different ways their sense could influence the situation, outcome, or result.

- **Seeing**   If the object was red instead of blue, if it were daylight instead of nighttime.

Noting how our senses stimulate different thoughts

- **Hearing**   If the eagle could have told the person what it heard, if the setting were prairie instead of deep forest, the sounds might have...

- **Taste**   If the character had not liked the taste of fish, if the diet were high in carbohydrates , if...

- **Touch**   If the person has reached out in the dark and felt cold instead of warmth, if the box was heavy and not light, if...

- **Smell**   If the wind were blowing their way, if the animal hadn't smelled the ____ , etc.

Having the student think through their senses serves to embed understanding of why things are the way they are - and how they can be altered.

Sensory ~ 30 *Altering Sensory Input*

Gaining New Perspectives Through the Senses

Teacher Generated

We all receive stimuli through our senses. If asked to ascertain how other or altered senses might change things, we use both internal and external references to examine something. Being aware of our senses and how they influence our perception of things can help us understand ourselves and others.

Considering multiple sensory options as we survey information can help broaden perspective, transfer of emotion, and ideation to other, previously not thought of areas.

1. Have students explore alternative senses as they contemplate a time in history, a character in a novel, a process depicting a flow from beginning to end, or a formula for determining a slope, graph, or other representation. For example:

    ▪ "When you think of _____'s character, what type of music do you think s/he'd prefer?

    ▪ What foods would be his/her preference?"

    ▪ "How would this situation differ if it took place in a city? In the dark? If it were raining? "

    ▪ "What sensations do you think people felt while on a particular journey?"

    ▪ "What color would best suit this?"

Identifying imagery through varying sensory modalities

2. Each time, check to see how prevalent any categories of thought have emerged, and ask the students why they selected that music, that food, that setting, etc.

Link teaching practice with assessment practices.

3. When assessing students, be sure to have them reference such sensory perspectives, as they respond to the tasks provided.

4. Ask students which sense provided the strongest imagery in their mind.

Sensory ~ 31 Body in Space: The Earlobe Effect

Rote Memorization Through Body Positions

Student Generated

When someone simultaneously engages two or more of the natural learning systems, the potential to form multiple pathways (connections) increases. Multiple pathways provide additional access for recall.

All strategies require adaptations with consideration of the learners, the setting, and the instructor.

The age or setting of students will determine their level of willingness to engage in various types of movement. You will need to modify both the movement and the application presented here to fit the age group and the content you are addressing.

Simultaneous use of the Cognitive, Social, and Physical Learning Systems.

1. While practicing a rote set of facts or other information that is organized into groups or categories, have learners touch their left index finger to their left ear lobe. For example:

    ▪ While practicing your "2's" multiplication table with a peer, touch your left index finger to your left ear lobe as you say each fact.

      o "Two times two equals four, two times three equals six, etc."

Students generate body-mind positions they are comfortable using.

2. Have students select a different "body in space" condition for each multiplication table. For example:

    ▪ Cover your right eye when you recite the three's table.

    ▪ Touch your chin while you recite the four's table.

    ▪ While seated in your chair, position your right foot vertically so that only your toes touch the floor while reciting the five's table.

    ▪ and so on.

3. Remind students intermittently to practice their facts while using the body positions that have been designated for each.

Alternative pathways to recall information are accessed.

You may notice, during practice, a timed test, or as a learner works to solve a problem, that s/he approximates one of the positions. This may serve to enhance recall through an alternative pathway if the cognitive system is not accessed or preferred.

Sensory ~ 32 Moving to Sounds of Taste

Understanding Through Multiple Sensory Lens

Teacher Generated

When someone simultaneously engages two or more of the senses, opportunities for exploring multiple pathways for understanding and recall are formed.

All strategies require adaptations with consideration of the learners, the setting, and the instructor

The age or setting of students will determine their level of willingness to engage in various types of movement. You will need to modify how senses are engaged or the application presented here to fit the age group and the content you are addressing.

Simultaneous use of the Cognitive and Physical Learning Systems.

1. After reading a passage, section of a story, chapter in a textbook, or completing some other body of information, pause and ask students to depart from the convention of the cognitive learning system, and then engage the physical learning system through multiple senses.

Social Learning System.

2. Divide the class into as many groups as you have approaches. See example below:

3. Assign a sense to each group as you wish: sound, taste, touch, movement, etc.

Alternative pathways to recall information are accessed.

4. Ask each group to reconsider the designated material through the lens of their assigned sense.

   - The "sound" group might explore noises, sounds, or music that they believe would best "fit" the scene or information or context.

   - The "taste" group might explore foods, palettes, or diets of characters or peoples.

   - The "touch" group may align various movements, transportation factors, or sensitivities to climates from their lens.

5. After each group has developed their "sensory lens" have them share what they are thinking with the class.

6. During assessments, remind students of the sensory lenses discussed.

Mental ~ 33   Student Visualization: Inner Space Travel

Building on Stored Packets of Information

Teacher Generated

The mind stores information in "packets" that are comprised of both verbal and visual elements. When we "close our eyes" and think, we often "see" images or ideas in pictorial form. The brain naturally generated visual reference to new learning - seeking pattern, meaning, and contexts that are familiar. Having students actively consider mental images consciously draws upon existing networks of thought.

Drawing attention to key ideas sends a message to learners about its importance.

Select a key passage from a story, or a situation from the chapter, or a process that occurs in science.

Reducing the competition of other sensory input can help the mind to focus--and to consciously access stored information.

1.   Have students clear their workspace and sit facing you. Tell them you would like them to close their eyes and "visualize" as you read a passage. Ask them to pay careful attention to what "comes to mind" as they listen to the reading.

2.   Read the passage. For example:

Visualizing creates networks that can link ideas.

Emotional Learning System may be engaged as the conduit to recalling similar feelings in other, prior experiences

- "You decide to take a trip to the Channel Islands off the coast of California. As you arrive at the location and walk on to the beach, you note the sunny, clear and 80 degree day all about you. A mild breeze is blowing and you set your travel pack down. You pull your snorkel, fins and mask from the pack and walk to the water's edge to put them on."

"You slowly move into the ocean, feeling the cool water pour over your body, as you swim toward deeper waters. You see schools of silver fish, hundreds of them, swirling about. Small yellow and black striped fish poke about the rocks and vegetation as a dark, large image streaks toward you. It nears in seconds and you identify it as a seal."

3. Ask students to open their eyes and write any words down that come to mind as they reflect on the reading and the imagery generated in their minds.

Internal Imagery makes up the majority of our composite processing...even with concrete visual inputs.

- Inquire about their experience. How did they elaborate on the setting,, the things they may have imagined or figuratively experienced, as they listened and formed scenarios?

Asking students to commit a thought, perspective, or hypothesis to paper helps to activate thinking and foster greater participation.

- Note similarities and differences between how students responded. Similarities will likely abound. Differences stem from the variety of experiences each individual has stored and "connects" to as they listen and conjure meaning in pictorial form (prior experimental knowledge).

- Some will have positive reactions to the entire reading, some will be mixed, and some (perhaps non-swimmers) will react with anxiety. All stems from what has previously been stored in the brain.

Using mental imagery requires the learner to explore his/her experiences and dispositions relative to a topic. As a pre-unit experience, it can provide a link to personal interest or meaning. It may also construct "networks" that can aid in creating neural connections as well as prompt more recall cues.

4. From this point, you have many options. You can:

- Use their personal imagery as a writing prompt.

- Have them explore similarities/differences between their experience and the experience of a character they are reading about.

- Create a "map" of their ideas and sensations to use as they engage with the upcoming marine life unit.

- Have students generate a drawing of their mental image.

5. Assign homework requiring students to involve others in sharing a related experience. For example:

Reflective Learning System

- Have them ask a parent about an episode at the beach or in the ocean that paralleled the dominant emotion they felt while listening to the reading.

Mental ~ 34 *Visualizing Words into Images and Actions*

Learning New Vocabulary Words Through Stored Packets of Information

Teacher Generated

The mind stores information in "packets" that are comprised of both verbal and visual elements. When we pay conscious attention, we notice that words generate mental images in the brain. Having students deliberately link mental images, words, and actions as they reflect on vocabulary or concepts creates relationships in the mind that, if tended, can establish long term memory.

Inviting learners to actively link words/ideas in their mind in a conscious manner can serve to link networks for greater recall.

Select vocabulary from the chapter, unit, text or other appropriate sources, that the students will encounter frequently over the next week or two. If desired, students may select the words. It may be best to start by using only 3 or 4 pairs of words at first.

1. Pair words together. They do not have to be obviously related, in fact you may want to avoid connecting "like" words - as they cause interference with one another. See the list below as an example.

Visualizing meaning, image, and interaction, as well as using novelty in the process creates links that enhance memory and retrieval cues.

Italy	**Tree**
Roman	**Steel**
Gods	**Vessel**
Roads	**Horses**
Chariot	**Feasts**
War	**Architecture**
Columns	**Robes**
Coliseum	**Scholars**

Internal Imagery makes up the majority of our composite processing, even with concrete visual inputs.

Asking students to commit a thought, perspective, or hypothesis to paper helps to activate thinking and foster greater participation.

2. Tell students that this is a "do your own work" exercise. You will say each pair of words and then pause 3-5 seconds.

- Ask them to hear the pair of words and then create mental imagery with them.

- Tell them to have the two items interact in any manner they wish - plain or absurd - real or in ways that are not possible. In other words, be playful with representations of the two words and their meanings/images. For example:
  - Italy & Tree: One could visualize the "boot" shape of the country kicking a tree and the tree saying "ouch," and the tree picking up the boot and tossing it high in the air.

3. Read each pair, allowing 3-5 seconds for each to be processed. When done, ask students to write down as many word pairs as they can recall.

4. Check to see which ones were recalled more than others.

5. Ask students to share their imagery - how they "saw" the objects interacting in their minds.

   - It may be that the words less frequently recalled need more descriptors or references over the next two days, in order to help secure them in context and ultimately, in memory.

Using mental imagery requires the learner to explore his/her experiences and dispositions relative to a topic. When s/he takes discretionary action upon the items, the brain engages in ways that the more passive "word by definition" process does not employ.

6. From this point, you have many options. You can:

   - Have them write descriptors for each word missed - not definitions, but descriptive thoughts that link to the word as it relates to the unit of study.

   - Have them cut out images of the words from magazines and write synonyms or descriptors to accompany the picture.

   - Create a class map of word groupings that "go together."

Mental ~ 35 Imaginary Friends

Conversations with a Significant Imaginary Character

Teacher Generated

The mind stores information in "packets" that are comprised of both verbal and visual elements. When we "close our eyes" and think, we often imagine possibilities that we know are not, or will not take place, but that serve to explore thinking and options.

Putting yourself into another's shoes.

Tell students to put themselves in the place of a historical figure, a scientist, an inventor, or even another person they know.

- The objective of this activity will be different for "known" people than for more removed characters.

- Then provide them with a scenario or ask them to construct a scenario of interest to them.

Drawing on known information.

Interpreting beyond known information.

Building from context

1.   Have them imagine a conversation they would have, or that two characters might have with this person.

- Provide prompts, asking students to ask their imaginary interviewee:

    o   What does s/he thinks about the government, the state of the economy, or the social welfare of the populace.

    o   Consider the nature of mankind these days.

    o   Or, what they'd like for dinner!

2. Discuss the various elements that came into student's minds as they constructed the imaginary dialogue with the person.

    ■   Make a list of these elements and determine if general categories can be made:

        o   Technologies Available

        o   Cultural Factors

        o   Economics

        o   Political Realm

        o   Social Constraints

        o   Diet

        o   Knowledge Available at the Time

        o   And so forth.

Articulation of the rationale behind thinking makes learning more explicit.

Creating categories helps to anchor main ideas.

3. Ask the students to role play. Let one character be "out of sync" with the group or the times while all others must stay in character.

    ■   Note how the historic figures deal with ideas and statements that are not aligned with the thinking of their day.

Using mental imagery requires the learner to explore his/her experiences and dispositions relative to a topic.

4. Assign homework that requires students to involve others in sharing a related experience. For example:

    ■   Have the students ask a parent about their grandparents, and an unusual conversation they can recall that might demonstrate how people or their views have changed.

Reflective Learning System

Mental 36   Imagery Reading

Previewing Mental and Emotional Content

Student Generated

Creating a Reflective Learning System for students to use as they interact with new information.

The mind stores information in "packets" that are comprised of both verbal and visual elements. When we "close our eyes" and form a clear image from the text we have been viewing, the information and meaning blend into more stable, accessible memory packets.

Before reading a story or chapter, devise a template for students in some semblance of the following:

Drawing on known information.

Interpreting beyond known information.

Building from context

1. Leave a blank space at the top half of the paper with the following information in the bottom half:

Passage ratings: 1 = low   5 = high

Passage 1	Emotion	1	2	3	4	5
Passage 1	Keywords/Imagery	1	2	3	4	5
Passage 2	Emotion	1	2	3	4	5
Passage 2	Keywords/Imagery	1	2	3	4	5
Passage 3	Emotion	1	2	3	4	5
Passage 3	Keywords/Imagery	1	2	3	4	5

Explicitly asking students to form imagery has been shown to increase recall.

Explicitly having students identify emotional occurrences and key words helps to have them read with multiple purposes, thus intending multiple pathways for both processing and recall.

2. Have students read a page of text. Pre-readers will need the passage read to them. Before they turn the page, have them move their eyes to a blank piece of paper. Think about the page you just read and:

    ▪ Form a mental picture that represents something in that page.

    ▪ Rate the level of emotional activity that the passage "stirred" in you.

    ▪ Write down one or two key words and rate the extent of imagery the words form in their minds.

        ○ If writing is not viable, have the students express a key word and the teacher can write it down.

        ○ Only do about 4-5 for the entire class each time.

- ONLY DO THIS ABOUT 3 TIMES. The intent is to foster mental imagery, not to slow the process down for a long period of time. Do this intermittently during the chapter, story, or unit of study.

Feedback has been shown to be one of the most effective ways to improve learning outcomes.

Tracking student progress on discrete criteria helps them understand specifically what they need to focus on. Similarly, it serves teachers to know what instructional strategies have impact on learner achievement.

3. Intra-tracking impact: Keep track of the emotional ratings for each student over several passages. Then align their performance in relation to recall, or comprehension of information, or key ideas in those passages. It may be interesting to determine any relationship between rating, imagery activity, key words, and recall.

Inter-tracking impact: Keep track, just as above. However, this time, determine the differences (if any) between passages that have not been conducted in this manner and those which have.

Similar/different explorations are known to be extremely effective to embed learning.

Meaningful adult-child interactions are vital to life successes.

4. Ask students to take a passage home and have their parents form imagery, rate emotion and determine a keyword. See if the ratings and words chosen by parents are similar or different than the ones the class chose.

Mental ~ 37   Blending Imagery and Pictures Reading

Conversations with a Significant Imaginary Character

Teacher Generated

The mind stores information in "packets" that are comprised of both verbal and visual elements. When we "close our eyes" and form a clear image from the text we have been viewing, the information and meaning blend into more stable, accessible memory packets.

Creating opportunities for bimodal packets as students interact with new information.

Cut out several pictures or photographs from magazines or other sources. Take care to select a variety of both content and emotional tones. For example:

▪ Circumstances or expressions that cover a wide range of feelings, from peaceful to hectic to distressful to joyous.

Using pictures to elicit reactions from prior experiences.

Merging provided imagery with internal imagery.

1. Place multiple images around the room in view of all students.

Explicitly asking students to form imagery has been shown to increase recall.

1a. Show students a film, film clip, video, etc.

1b. Option: Have students read a passage, poem, or segment about an historical time, or you read one to them.

Explicitly having students identify emotional occurrences and key words helps to have them read with multiple purposes, thus intending multiple pathways for both processing and recall.

2. Ask students to reflect on a film segment or the passage, and decide upon a key term that comes to mind as they think about it. For example:

▪ Variations: disposition toward, feelings about, assessment of, etc.

3. Tell students to look about the room and locate a picture that they feel is most "aligned" with their thoughts and response to the film/passage.

4.   Ask students to form three lists of words as follows:

Words / feelings about the film or passage read	In Common	Words / feelings about the picture selected from the wall

Providing or establishing a template helps some students with the organization of information.

Social Learning System

5.   Have students place words that come to mind in each of the three sections first, then note words in common in the center.

6.   Pair students to share their ideas and agree on two or more items for each column.

Identifying with prior experiences

Accessing emotional tags

- If students selected different pictures, have them discuss why.

- Discuss what similarities they had in the **reasons** they selected each picture.

- Have the students, as willing or appropriate, share actual stories that generated their reaction.

Similarities and differences are powerful learning tools.

7.   Discuss as a class, the major impressions the passage induced in everyone.

8.   As appropriate, determine the top few.

Explicitly having students identify emotional occurrences helps to have them connect with prior experiences and develop emotional tags for memory.

9.   Ask volunteers about a key story or impression that was shared In their pairs work.

- Often, a story shared by a student will serve as a powerful cue for recall later in class work.

10.   Make any "links" between circumstances, impressions, and feelings generated to the content you are covering.

Mental ~ 38   *Connecting Imagery, Lines, and Disposition*

Blending Visual and Emotional Information

Studies show that the majority of "visual" activity in the brain originates from internal sources, prior experiences, and imagination, with subsequent input from external sources through our eyes. (Zemke).

Student Generated

Helping students identify or alter a mood can affect learning outcomes.

1. Provide each student with an 8 1/2 x 11 piece of paper.

2. Have the students fold the paper twice ~ once in each direction so they will have four boxes as shown below.

Creating opportunities for students to get in touch with their current emotional state or to access a more productive mindset.

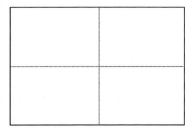

3. Have the students write the four words in the boxes, as shown below.

Calm/Peace	Anger
Joy	Frustration

4. One by one, have students focus on just one emotion/feeling, for example calm/peace.

Emotional Learning System

   ▪ Tell them to close their eyes and just "feel," sensing a time/place when they felt utter calm.

Reflective Learning System

Internal Imagery

5. After about a minute of focusing, tell them to draw in that space on the paper.

   - No words or recognizable shapes.

   - "Let your pencil move in any way you feel."

   - Keep concentrating on the feeling as you do."

Connecting with imagery

6. After about 2-3 minutes (or when they seem done), have them look at their lines/imagery.

Similar / Different Strategy

7. Ask them to compare theirs with two people around them.

8. Ask them to notice any similarities or differences.

Representations of feelings and emotions in "print" form can help students to realize the inner energy that exists when we have such dispositions. One way to help them connect internal feelings with attitudes/behaviors.

9. Discuss/list similarities on the board. Have all students notice that we have many things in common when our feelings are strong. There are typically several things in common among an entire group. For example:

   - **Calm or Peace** soft, light, flowing lines, horizontal parallels, sometimes wavy.

   - **Anger** dark, jagged lines with sharp points.

   - **Joy** wispy lines, wavy, often flowing from lower left to upper right - or horizontal.

   - **Frustration** crossing lines with multi-directions; like anger, but a bit less intense.

Identifying our inner dispositions (feelings/attitude) is a crucial step toward:

1. Acknowledging that we are feeling/acting as we are;

2. Understanding why we are feeling/acting as we are;

3. Initiating potential thought, activity or interventions toward more a productive disposition for the situation.

10. If the class agrees on one or two similar characteristics of a variety of emotions and feelings, then illustrate these characteristics and post them on the wall for all to see. Two applications come to mind:

   A. Connecting to curriculum: Ask students what a person or group of people might be sensing/feeling as they work with the chapter, period of time, or a character in a situation. Have them see if one of the illustrations on the wall makes sense.

   B. Connecting to personal behaviors: When a student is having difficulty with his/her interactions with others - or in paying attention, ask which illustration best portrays their current mood. From there, begin a discussion of why their personal "lines (energy)" are in that place and ultimately, how they can alter their energy (or how we can help them shift it to a more productive place).

Mental ~ 39   Post Recess Blues

Attitude and Behavior Modification Through Imagery

Student Generated

Helping students identify or alter a mood through imagery can help to alter attitudes and behaviors.

Creating opportunities for students to get in touch with their current emotional state or to access a more productive mindset.

When a student returns from recess, another class, lunch, or arrives at school with an unproductive disposition it is difficult to proceed with the curriculum and learning.

A known place to go to work out internal issues

1. Create a FOCUS center - a space (corner, box, etc.) where students can go or are asked to visit when they are unable to focus on the learning task(s) requested of them. This is not "time-out," rather, this is an active, concerted effort to realign one's internal disposition to a more productive one.

2. Instruct all students about the FOCUS center and its uses and purpose. Have them practice the steps below as a class, so that they understand the procedure and also, that they respect anyone who is using the FOCUS center.

3. As you notice a student arrive with an "internal" conflict or with a distracting disposition (to him/herself or to others), ask him/her to sit quietly in the "focus center."

Linking words, feelings and imagery. Imagery is a powerful source of feelings.

Focusing on a "feeling" for one or more minutes can help to shift our disposition.

4. Several options are provided in the center, that are appropriate for differing student dispositions/entry points, such as: Joy, Calm, Friendship, Forgiveness, etc. Words, with imagery that aligns with them, that students will focus upon.

   ▪ Under the word, "Calm:" have a tranquil picture of water, a sunset or other images that the class feels capture that feeling.

   ▪ Under the word "Friendship," could be images of people getting along, hugging, being pals, one person with their arm around another in a supportive manner.

   ▪ Do the same for each word you have chosen.

Emotional Learning System	5. The student then gets a piece of paper and pencil. Before writing anything on the paper, s/he returns to focus on the image until s/he "feels" similar to what the imagery projects.
Reflective Learning System **Internal Imagery**	6. Once they have aligned with the imagery, they "draw" lines, in any fashion they feel. There should be no letters, numbers or shapes that are recognizable - just lines.

7. Behind the process: Identifying our inner dispositions (feelings/attitude) is a crucial step toward:

1) Acknowledging that we are feeling/acting as we are.

2) Connecting to personal behaviors:

Connecting emotion with imagery.

Representations of feelings and emotions in "print" form can help students to realize the inner energy that exists when we have such dispositions. One way to help them connect internal feelings with attitudes/behaviors.

- When a student is having difficulty with his/her interactions with others - or in paying attention, ask which illustration best portrays their current mood.

- From there, begin a discussion of why their personal "lines (energy)" are in that place and ultimately, how they can alter their energy (or how we can help them shift it to a more productive place.)

3) Initiating potential thought, activity or interventions toward a more productive disposition for the situation.

Mental ~ 40   Storying Concepts and Analogy ~ Visualizing Past Experiences

Personal Stories as a Basis for Analogy and Recall

Student Generated

Personal stories are a great source of prior knowledge - emotional "wells." Linking the meaning embedded in personal experiences with stories that emanate from learners serves to create a visual basis for memory.

Creating opportunities for students to get in touch with their experiences, referencing them with new learnings, is a primary way to instill long-term memory.

1. Illustrate or describe an essential concept or idea that the students will encounter in the upcoming lessons or unit of study, and generate an analogy to life experiences. For example:

    - The Pythagorean Theorem: A2 + B2 = C2... or... knowledge of two parts can help create understanding of a third part.

Pulling experiences from one's past in an effort to establish similarities with a new idea or concept helps to anchor the new learning in relation to an existing memory. Transfer is more likely.

Social Learning System.

2. Give students a few minutes to work with a partner and share personal, actual stories about their lives that parallel the concept or big idea presented by the teacher. They should tell each other specific aspects of the situation that are similar to the overall idea(s) represented in the concept.

Identifying with others on an emotional or experiential level crates memory paths that typically have more strength and are readily referenced.

3. Have students select stories to share with the class (orally). Have them exchange several. Often, one or more will resonate with the class such that they can easily identify with the circumstance.

Storying personalizes the learning experience.

4. When a story emerges that the class can identify with, you have a reference "anchor" to use each time the class could benefit from being reminded of the essential idea or concept that new information is about.

    - Many times, a story that emanates from the class will help all learners to better remember the main idea that has been presented, as it has been personalized for them.

Mental ~ 41 *Dawning Yesterday ~ Visualizing Yesterday, Today*

Prior Experiences
Capturing the Essence
of Learning

Student Generated

Recall is enhanced with imagery. Capturing prior learning and understandings through mental imagery can help generate the context for greater learning capacity.

Creating opportunities for students to use imagery to recall prior experiences helps to provide a context for additional experiences.

1. Start the day (class) by asking students to reflect on yesterday's activities (in general or in a specific subject). Students may close their eyes or just sit quietly and reflect on the prior day's learning.

Synthesis converging on the essence of meaning can be difficult, yet when achieved, provides the foundation for further understanding and transfer.

2. Tell students that you are not asking them to recall a list of facts or body of knowledge. Rather, you want them to synthesize the last class with them into a main idea, concept, thought - that can be captured as an image, or the "essence" of yesterday.

Capturing ideas, thoughts and feelings can happen in multiple ways.

3. Tell students to doodle, draw or create images on a blank paper, if they feel inclined - as they reflect on yesterday's activities.

Summarizing main ideas and concepts prior to moving forward with new curriculum helps the brain to locate connections and build meaning. It also provides opportunity for maintaining short-term memory while a learner works to grasp more understanding.

4. Class discussion or sharing:

    ▪ Ask students to offer the ideas and thoughts that came to mind. There may be a common theme or thread in their ideas, or their reflections may provide a wide range of recall areas.

    ▪ Either way, the review generates a summary of prior experience and knowledge that sets the stage for additional activity and learning.

Mental ~ 42   From Dusk to Dawn ~ Today's Reflection, Tonight's Memory

Reflection Leading to Consolidated Long-Term Memory

Student Generated

Reflection is a powerful tool for enhancing memory and recall. What occurs first (primacy) and last (recency) have a natural tendency for greater recall. Pausing to reflect on what took place, what meaning may have formed and so forth, preempts the deep sleep of the upcoming night - when the brain undergoes chemical changes and works to consolidate (strengthen) memory.

Creating opportunities for students to use imagery to reflect at the end of the day/class.

1. End the day (class) by asking students to reflect on today's learning (in general or in a specific subject). Students may close their eyes or just sit quietly and reflect on the day's (class) activities.

2. Take two minutes and have students offer "big ideas" and essential understandings that they derived from today's class. As students share, write the ideas (in abbreviated form as necessary) on the board.

Timely reflection helps the brain to organize and recall the big ideas to which detail ultimately becomes connected.

3. After several ideas are on the board for all to see, ask students if any of the ideas "go together" or have things in common. Connecting ideas will form quasi-categories that should reflect the intended major learnings of the day.

Timely feedback--RIGHT NOW--goes a long way toward correcting misconceptions.

4. The teacher has an opportunity at this time to acknowledge accurate conceptions or to correct misunderstandings. This strategy provides immediate feedback about what the students are considering important and how they see the learning.

   ▪ If the "class" is on target - this reinforces their understanding.

   ▪ If the "class" is off-base from what the teacher sees as important - then this input will serve to help refocus the next lesson to assure accuracy of understandings.

Deep sleep is one facet of the physical learning system that learners need to "secure" learning in memory.

5. Finally, when people enter deep sleep periods, the brain's "chemical soup" converts from an aminergic state to a cholinergic state.

   ▪ The choline based environment served to "revisit" and consolidate the activity of the day.

   ▪ In effect, it strengthens or deletes neural connections - impacting long term memory.

SECTION SEVEN *Nonlinguistic Representation Organizers*

Instructional Notes

Templates and Organizers Overview

The following pages include a series of organizers for a variety of uses. As presented, they require adaptations to match variations in learner abilities, to specific purpose, and to the scope of the content to be addressed. In some cases, additional notes have been made to clarify steps and content.

Please feel free to reproduce these organizers for use with your own students. Also, please take the time necessary to make any adjustments in their format or content to customize them to the specific demands of the assignments you will provide - as well as the learning needs of the students you have in mind.

Unit Planner: Multipurpose

Assignment and Variations

This organizer intends to prompt thinking about aspects of an upcoming unit that will be important for a student to keep in mind - elements that will support organization, memory, and ultimate learning. Components may be altered to suit any specific unit of study and its commensurate objectives aimed at what a learner must know and be able to do as a result of the unit.

Unit Name or Title

Primary Concept or Essential Question

Main Ideas and Components

1. _____
2. _____
3. _____
4. _____
5. _____

Key FACTS, Knowledge, or Process Components

Critical Vocabulary

1. _____
2. _____
3. _____
4. _____
5. _____
6. _____
7. _____
8. _____

Additional Vocabulary

1. _____
2. _____
3. _____
4. _____
5. _____
6. _____
7. _____

Teacher Example

Student Example

Analogy / Metaphor

Memory, Recall, the Brain & Learning

Unit Planner: Procedural Knowledge

Unit Name or Title

Primary Concept or
Essential Question

**Main Idea, Goal, or
Procedure**

INITIAL Status

FIRST Step
SECOND Step
THIRD Step
FOURTH Step
FIFTH Step
SIXTH Step
SEVENTH Step

FINAL Status

Unit Planner: Declarative Knowledge

Unit Name or Title

Primary Concept or
Essential Question

Main Ideas

FACTS	Fiction	FACTS	Fiction	FACTS	Fiction
1.		1.		1.	
2.		2.		2.	
3.		3.		3.	
4.		4.		4.	
5.		5.		5.	
6.		6.		6.	

Vocabulary Development

Assignment and Variations

This template is organized to prompt learner exploration of meaning prior to any exposure to or attempt to converge on a definition.

- identifying descriptors
- words that help to explain
- words or phrases that support or provide context
- words that help describe - provide a basis for understanding that will build meaning around an idea
- concept or new vocabulary term

Begin this template at the top, as a class discussion, having students locate images/photos (middle-left) for homework or to create drawings that result from the discussion. Only after the top two sections are complete will a definition better be processed for longer-term memory and transfer.

Descriptor	The Word or Concept			Descriptor
	Descriptor	Descriptor	Descriptor	

Picture or Photo

Student Generated Drawing or Illustration

Definition ~ filled out last

Cypress Vocabulary

Conjugations | Word | Chapter

Part of Speech

Make Up a Story with the Word in it | List Definitions

Draw a Picture of the Word

Synonyms | Examples: | How I Am Going to Remember the Word

Antonyms

This Organizer was designed by Kimberly Carraway from the Carraway Center for Teaching and Learning

Summarizing for Definition

Assignment Describe a concept and identify subordinate ideas using the process pattern below. Then have students work as a team to generate analogous information for topic/subject area that you have selected.

1. Identify the subject to be defined or studied.

The Word or Concept

For Example: Mosquito

2. Identify the general category the subject belongs to.

Category

For Example: Insects

This portion may be done as a group/team/pairs initially, then discussed as a whole class.

3. List characteristics of the subject that separate it from other items in the same general category.

For Example
- Six Legs
- Brown
- Flies
- Makes High Pitched Sound

This portion may be done as a group/team/pairs initially, then discussed as a whole class.

4. List different or related types of the selected subject.

For Example
What are the types of insects that extract blood from other animals?

Chapter Book Reading Summary

As You Begin

Draw a picture of the main characters.

Character Names _____ _____ _____

Draw a picture of the setting and the problem.

Describe the problem. _____
_____
_____
_____

Chapter _____

Draw a picture of the main event in the chapter and write one sentence to describe it.

_____
_____
_____

List three important details that describe the event the order they appeared.

1. _____
2. _____
3. _____

What was the importance of this event? _____
_____

When did this event happen in the timeline of the story? _____

This Organizer was designed by Laura Paull and Doris Wells-Papanek© 2004

Visual Notetaker

name   **date**

Write/draw a mind map, or illustrate the content you are summarizing.

Based on the summary above, what are the big ideas?	big idea	big idea	big idea
Now expand on each of them.	expand	expand	expand
What are the important details?	details	details	details

notes	questions	connections and reactions
_____	_____	_____
_____	_____	_____
_____	_____	_____
_____	_____	_____
_____	_____	_____

This Organizer was designed by Doris Wells-Papanek © 2004

Brainstorming Ideas

topic   date

Write words or phrases that come to mind when you think about the general topic.

Write details that come to mind about the topic.

Now write or draw 3 possible categories that can be formed from the above list.

Use a different colored pencil or highlighter to identify each category and the related details.

This Organizer was designed by Doris Wells-Papanek and Laura Paull © 2004

129

Draw A Storyboard

story   **date**

Draw an image to illustrate the topic of the story and its events.

Draw a series of images to describe the important components of the story and its events.

This Organizer was designed by Doris Wells-Papanek © 2004

Writing Body Paragraphs with Post-It's

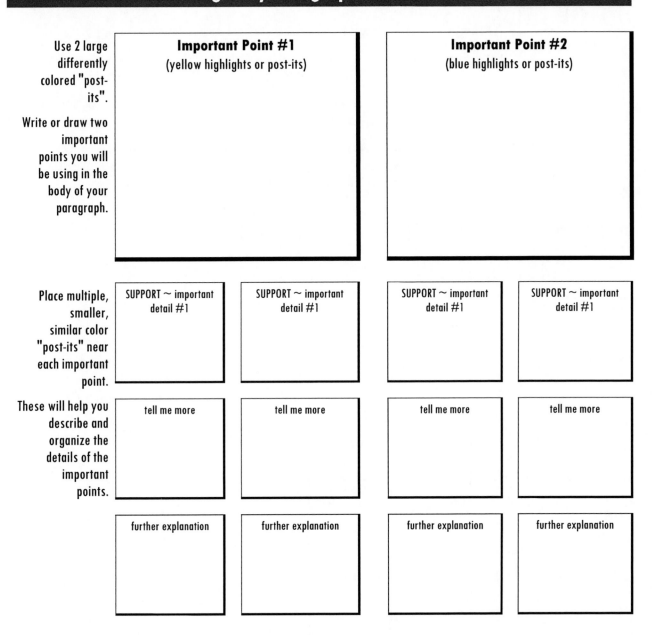

Use 2 large differently colored "post-its".

Write or draw two important points you will be using in the body of your paragraph.

Important Point #1
(yellow highlights or post-its)

Important Point #2
(blue highlights or post-its)

Place multiple, smaller, similar color "post-its" near each important point.

These will help you describe and organize the details of the important points.

SUPPORT ~ important detail #1	SUPPORT ~ important detail #1	SUPPORT ~ important detail #1	SUPPORT ~ important detail #1
tell me more	tell me more	tell me more	tell me more
further explanation	further explanation	further explanation	further explanation

This Organizer was designed by Laura Paull and Doris Wells-Papanek © 2004

Prompt, Condition, and Explanation

Prompt	Give the class a situation that you want them to explore more fully
Condition	Option 1) Ask them to consider various conditions (temperature, climate, people, location, politics, era, etc.) that might impact the situation
	Option 2) Provide various conditions that you want them to consider in relation to the prompt item
Explanation	Have the class generate explanation of what they think exists under this circumstance, will happen, or other outcomes. This requires learners to examine the influences of variables on a circumstance, object, or person.

Prompt Item	Condition	Explanation or Thoughts
1	1	1
2	2	2
3	3	3
4	4	4

Story Events

Assignment

Provide basic categories that prompt students to "look" for information can help them identify main ideas and details that serve to organize information for later use in projects, writing, and other appropriate purposes. The number of major topics will vary by unit and could include one or more that students select.

Title of the Story, Event, or Item

History

Geography

Characters

1. _____

2. _____

1. _____

2. _____

1. _____

2. _____

Analogies

Example

basis word	tree	**is to**	leaf
as	mall	**is to**	store

Relationship Both basis words provide the architecture to hold inter-components together.

basis word		**is to**	
as		**is to**	

Relationship _____

basis word		**is to**	
as		**is to**	

Relationship _____

basis word		**is to**	
as		**is to**	

Relationship _____

Compare and Contrast Comparison Matrix Chart

Assignment This template aligns with the #1 strategy for student achievement a la Marzano et. al. It captures the simple dichotomy of differences and similarities between items across as many elements as you wish learners to explore.

Item for Comparison Conifers: any tree that has thin leaves or needles and produces cones ~ many are evergreen, such as pines, firs, junipers, larches, spruces, and yews.

Characteristics	1. needles	2. foliage	3. shape
1. Similarities	most are green	drop needles in fall	mostly conical
Differences	length of needles	some drop all	tall vs. short
2. Similarities			
Differences			
3. Similarities			
Differences			
4. Similarities			
Differences			
5. Similarities			
Differences			

Classification Comparison Matrix Chart

Assignment Ask students, or as teachers, or both, please fill out the top row of categories for sorting information. As the information is complete in each organizer, place items in each category, and then add criteria for being "included" in the category that should be identified in the middle (second) section. The criteria may be determined ahead of time - or developed as items are placed in each category.

Items for Categorization	1.	2.	3.	4.
Criteria for Inclusion ~ Rules	*	*	*	*
	*	*	*	*
	*	*	*	*
	*	*	*	*

Identified Components, Elements, and Items for Inclusion

Point of View

Assignment

This template prompts varied points of view. The learner(s) must look at an issue or issues from many angles, which you can alter according to your topic or unit of study. It serves as a means of having students gather and record their ideas.

ISSUE: How Would Life Be Different, If there were NO...	Explain
Common Currency (coins, bills, money $$$)	
Vehicles for Transportation	
Friends	
Laws	
Books or Magazines	
Email	
Internet	
Telephone	
Television	

Changing Things ~ For or Against?

Assignment

This template provides organization for thoughts or ideas as individual or groups of students explore an issue. It is a basis for further discuss or for the formation of an overall disposition toward an issue.

Big Idea:

Q: How would things be different if there were no bed times or curfews?

Q: What would it be like to live in _____ ?

For example: country, a time in history, or different climate.

Things that would be DIFFERENT

1.
2.
3.
4.
5.
6.
7.

Which would you choose?

Keep the SAME	Make it DIFFERENT

Why?

Things that would be the SAME

1.
2.
3.
4.
5.
6.

Pro-Con Issue Deliberation

Assignment

This template is vital for developing the organization necessary for a thesis statement or argument position. It helps learners think about main ideas and support details for the main ideas. As they organize or prioritize the details, in order of importance to the support of a position (either side), they begin to develop the structure for their thesis and how to prepare a conclusion regarding their position.

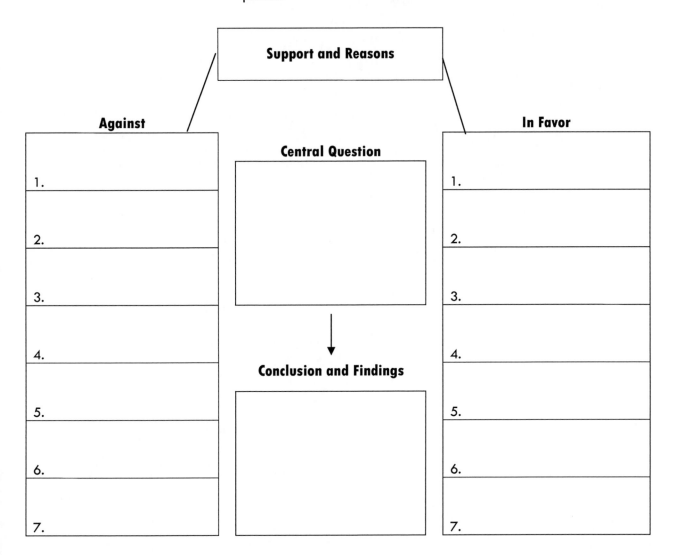

Support and Reasons

Against

1.

2.

3.

4.

5.

6.

7.

Central Question

Conclusion and Findings

In Favor

1.

2.

3.

4.

5.

6.

7.

Process ~ Cause and Effect Patterns

Assignment

Cause and effect templates help learners track the order of events and the role one element plays on another. The chronology of a series of events/elements is placed in will greatly impact thinking and ultimate conclusions.

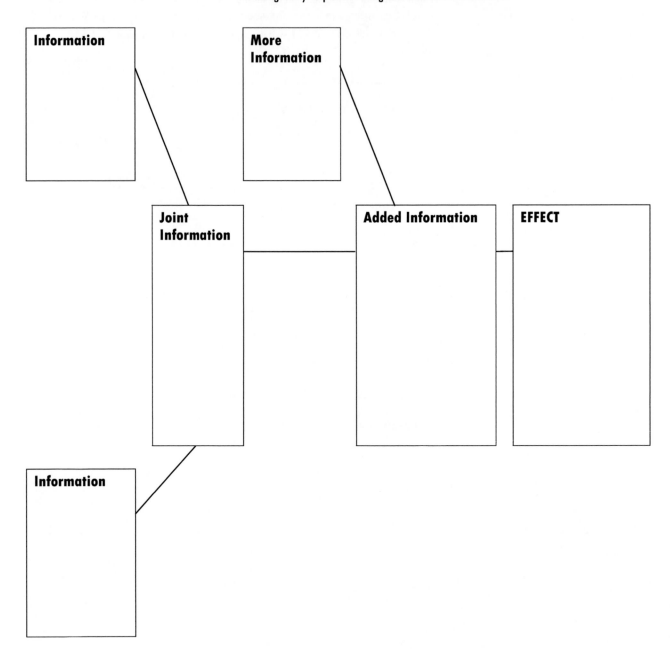

The Chronology of Cause and Effect

Assignment

1. Use the sequence below to record the order of events, as you understand them.

2. Start with the first known event (cause), then move upward to the right and note any impact (effect) that took place resulting from the first event.

3. With each successive step, continue to record that takes place after each event. Number each below the diagram (sequence) so that the chronology is depicted.

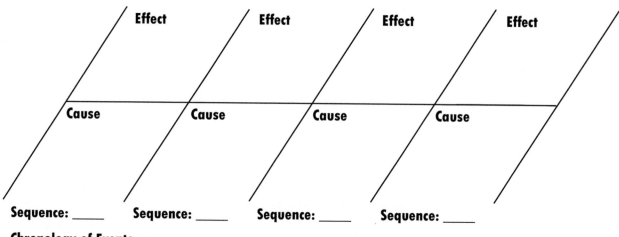

Chronology of Events

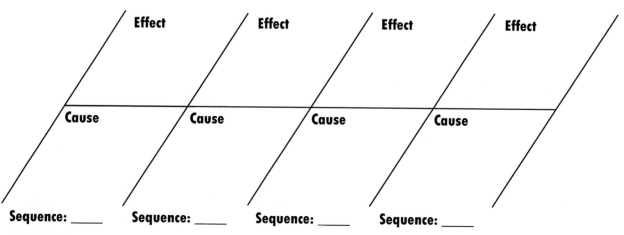

Chronology of Events

Summarizing to Prepare for an Argument

Assignment   Identify information to support an assertion, an assumption, or a claim. Have students work as a team to restate the claim in a manner to reduce the number of limitations.

The statement to be examined is:

1. Take a stand on an issue or write down a point of view that you believe is true, accurate, or representative of a circumstance, subject, or object.

What information would help you understand more about this?

2. What evidence or data do you have to support the claim?

Under what circumstances or criteria does the claim become less powerful? Does it have a flaw?

3. What limitations does the claim have?

Now, what do you think?

4. Which side of the argument would you prefer to be on?

Summarizing to Prepare for Problem Solving

Assignment   When a problem is introduced and more than one solution is derived.

- Have the students fill out 1. and 2a.
- Then have the students work in pairs to complete 2b.
- In teams of 4, have them revisit and complete 2a, b, and c.
- Finally, discuss and solve for 3 and 4.

1. The situation or circumstance that presents a problem is:

2a. One possible solution to this problem is:

2b. Another possible solution to this problem is:

2c. A third possible solution to this problem is:

3. Which solution has the best chance of succeeding?

4. Why?

Narrative Story Planner ~ Introduction, Characters, and Script

story name | **date**

opening event imagery ~ set the stage	conclusion restate point of the story and the significance of the event
	impact of event
	internal lesson learned from event
introduce main event	external lesson learned from event
purpose of the story, why important	
tone/mood	
date, day, time	event's affect on daily life
place	
colors	
sequence in time	

characters

name	name	name	name	name
1 imagery	2 imagery	3 imagery	4 imagery	5 imagery
attributes	attributes	attributes	attributes	attributes

story script

sequence #1	sequence #2	sequence #3	sequence #4	sequence #5
sequence #6	sequence #7	sequence #8	sequence #9	sequence #10

This Think-Sheet was designed by Doris Wells-Papanek © 2004

Narrative Story Planner ~ Sequence and Elaboration

story name   date

INTRODUCTION sensory imagery	see	character's feelings	affect on others
	hear	1	
	smell	2	
	taste	3	
	touch	4	
	tone/mood	5	

why important ? _____

BODY ONE sensory imagery	see	character's feelings	affect on others
	hear	1	
	smell	2	
	taste	3	
	touch	4	
	tone/mood	5	

why important ? _____

BODY TWO sensory imagery	see	character's feelings	affect on others
	hear	1	
	smell	2	
	taste	3	
	touch	4	
	tone/mood	5	

why important ? _____

CONCLUSION sensory imagery	see	character's feelings	affect on others
	hear	1	
	smell	2	
	taste	3	
	touch	4	
	tone/mood	5	

why important ? _____

This Think-Sheet was designed by Doris Wells-Papanek © 2004

Gathering New Information

Assignment This graphic provides an example of what a schemata could look like for students to capture and build relationships between ideas and information. As they create, fill in, or alter their "map" of information, the representation of their understanding can be viewed readily, helping them to note gaps or overlaps or strengths of thought and connection. For Example: the "Creating a Theme" map can be created by a student or a class.

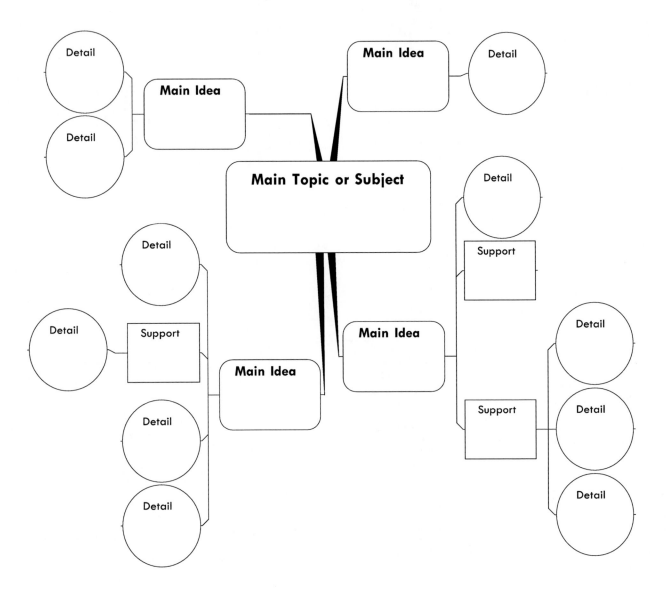

Episodic Patterns

Note The Episodic Patterns Mind Map could be used in concert with the Cause and Effects Organizers in the Content Organizers section.

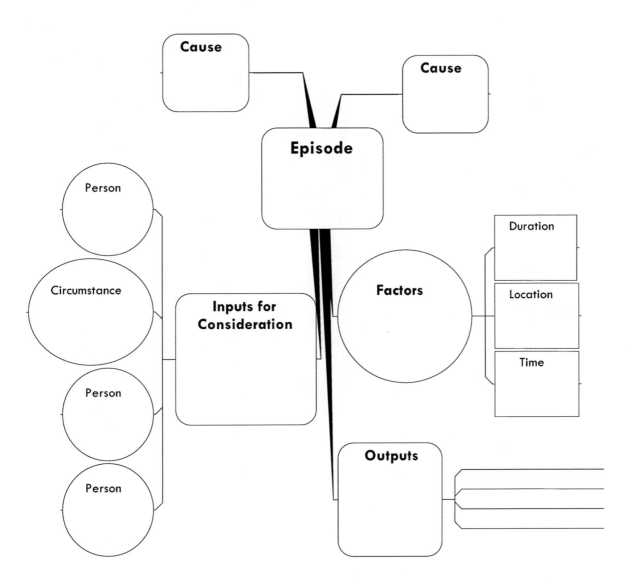

Creating Through a Theme ~ 1

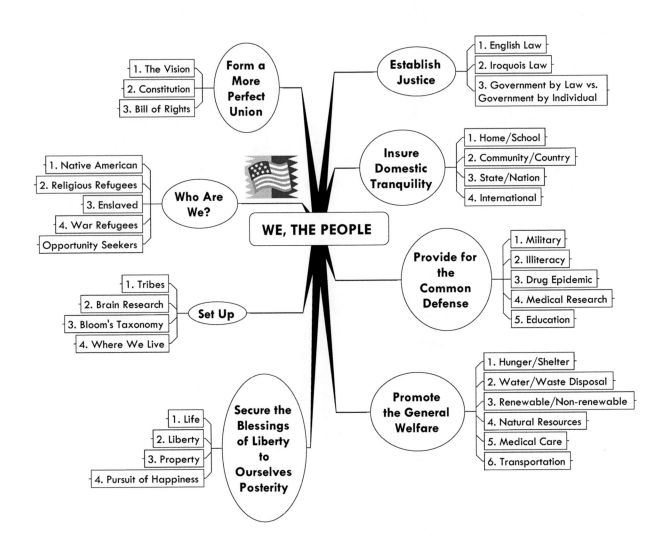

Form a More Perfect Union
1. The Vision
2. Constitution
3. Bill of Rights

Establish Justice
1. English Law
2. Iroquois Law
3. Government by Law vs. Government by Individual

Who Are We?
1. Native American
2. Religious Refugees
3. Enslaved
4. War Refugees
Opportunity Seekers

Insure Domestic Tranquility
1. Home/School
2. Community/Country
3. State/Nation
4. International

WE, THE PEOPLE

Set Up
1. Tribes
2. Brain Research
3. Bloom's Taxonomy
4. Where We Live

Provide for the Common Defense
1. Military
2. Illiteracy
3. Drug Epidemic
4. Medical Research
5. Education

Secure the Blessings of Liberty to Ourselves Posterity
1. Life
2. Liberty
3. Property
4. Pursuit of Happiness

Promote the General Welfare
1. Hunger/Shelter
2. Water/Waste Disposal
3. Renewable/Non-renewable
4. Natural Resources
5. Medical Care
6. Transportation

This Organizer was designed by Kovalik and Olsen © 2002

Creating Through a Theme ~ 2

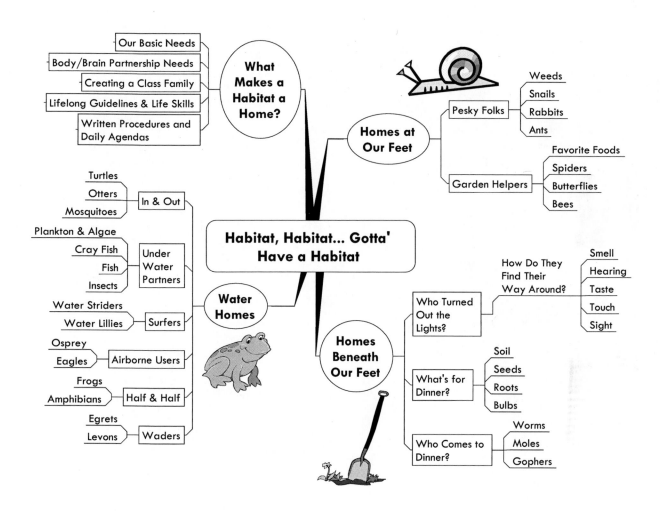

This Organizer was designed by Kovalik and Olsen © 2002

Classification ~ Cluster Schematic: Portrait

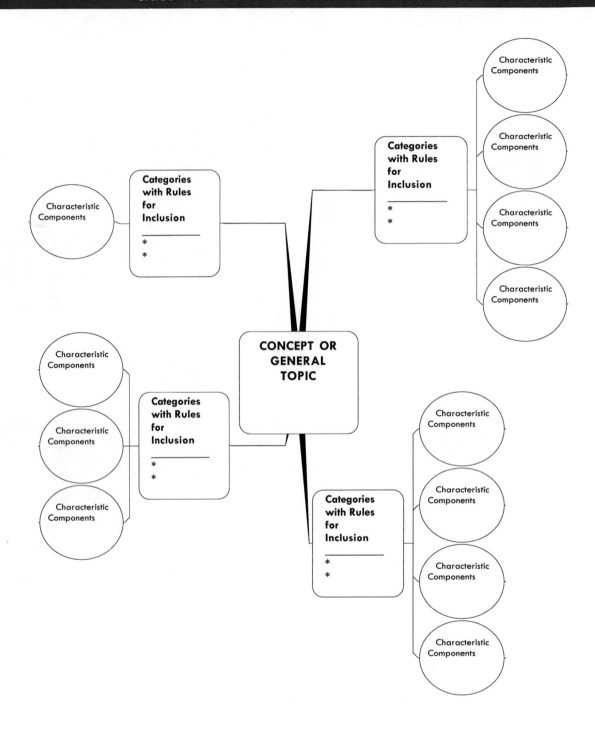

Classification ~ Cluster Schematic: Landscape

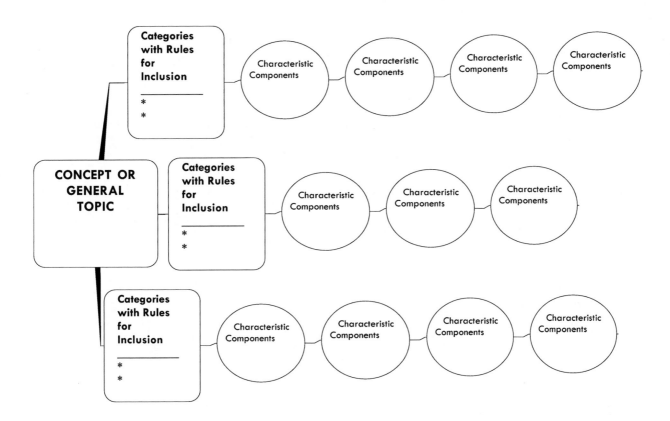

Different Learning Patterns ~ Sequential vs. Spatial Order

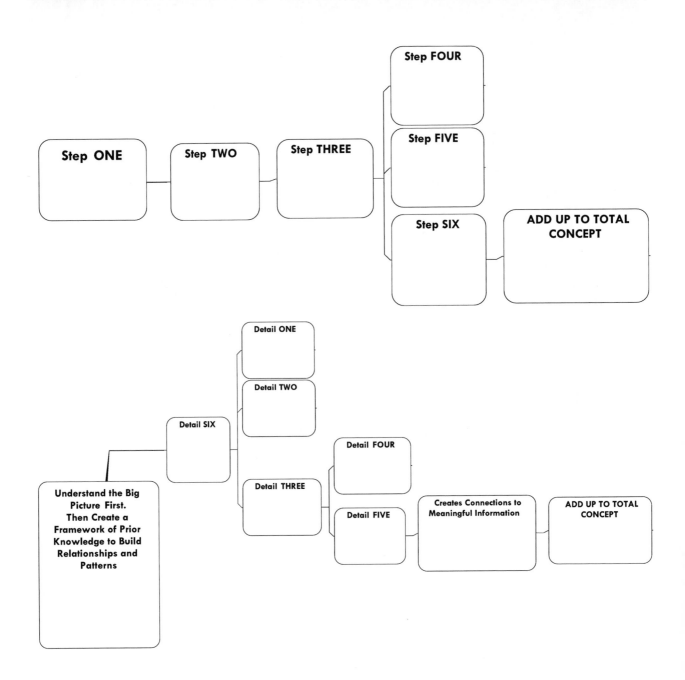

This Organizer was designed by Doris Wells-Papanek © 2004

Alpha~Math Steps

Assignment Please use an example to show "steps" and alpha explanations. Mathematics has three languages, that of alpha (words), numeric (numbers) and symbols. As such, a template requiring students to use two or more of these languages in conjunction with each other can help learners link the "languages" of mathematics. If symbols are also associated with each or any step, they could also be added to the template.

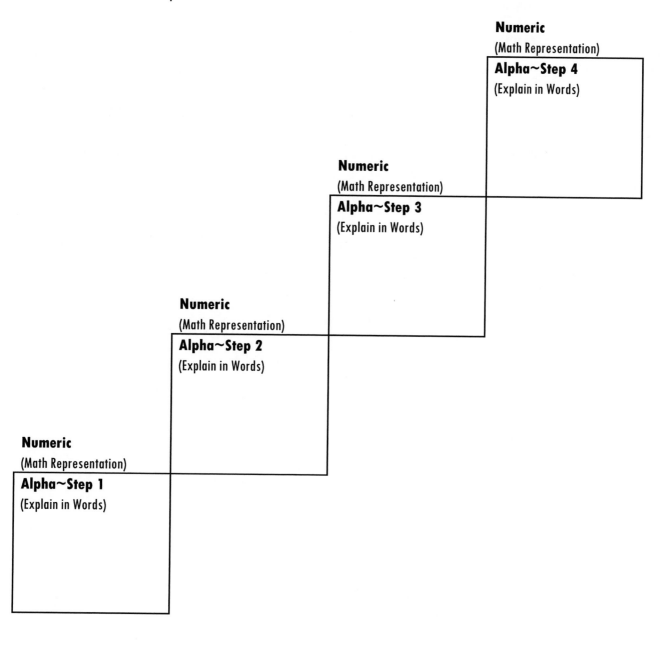

Numeric
(Math Representation)

Alpha~Step 4
(Explain in Words)

Numeric
(Math Representation)

Alpha~Step 3
(Explain in Words)

Numeric
(Math Representation)

Alpha~Step 2
(Explain in Words)

Numeric
(Math Representation)

Alpha~Step 1
(Explain in Words)

Exploring New Math Concepts

Assignment   This template is intended to segment components of any new math/science algorithm, formula, or process. It will require modification to your objective of study. An example follows.

New Concept, Relationships, or Ideas to be Explored

	Item 1	Item 2	Item 3	Item 3
Meaning ~ Personal Example from Experience				
Formal Definition				

Concept Explanation or Definition

Example of Concept or Idea

Exploring New Math Concepts

New Concept, Relationships, or Ideas to be Explored

Slope / Intercept /Form

	Item 1	Item 2	Item 3	Item 4
	Slope	Intercept	Form	
Meaning ~ Personal Example from Experience	The grade or how steep the ski mountain is	A football is being passed and received. (two objects crossing paths)	* A set way of doing things * A procedure or steps * Application	
Formal Definition	$$\dfrac{Rise}{Run}$$ $$\dfrac{Y_2 - Y_1}{X_2 - X_1}$$	Where the X & Y axis cross	A set way of setting up mathematical information	

Concept Explanation or Definition

The slope-intercept-form of the equation of a line with slope "m" and y-intercept "b" is $y = mx + b$

Example of Concept or Idea

$y = 3x + 4$ (or $y = y = mx + b$)

slope = m = 3

y-intercept = b = 4

Visual Multiplication Table by the Rules

	0	1	2	3	4	5	6	7	8	9	10
0	0x0=0	1x0=0	2x0=0	3x0=0	4x0=0	5x0=0	6x0=0	7x0=0	8x0=0	9x0=0	10x0=0
1	0x1=0	1x1=1	2x1=2	3x1=3	4x1=4	5x1=5	6x1=6	7x1=7	8x1=8	9x1=9	10x1=10
2	0x2=0	1x2=2	2x2=4	3x2=6	4x2=8	5x2=10	6x2=12	7x2=14	8x2=16	9x2=18	10x2=20
3	0x3=0	1x3=3	2x3=6	3x3=9	4x3=12	5x3=15	6x3=18	7x3=21	8x3=24	9x3=27	10x3=30
4	0x4=0	1x4=4	2x4=8	3x4=12	4x4=16	5x4=20	6x4=24	7x4=28	8x4=32	9x4=36	10x4=40
5	0x5=0	1x5=5	2x5=10	3x5=15	4x5=20	5x5=25	6x5=30	7x5=35	8x5=40	9x5=45	10x5=50
6	0x6=0	1x6=6	2x6=12	3x6=18	4x6=24	5x6=30	6x6=36	7x6=42	8x6=48	9x6=54	10x6=60
7	0x7=0	1x7=7	2x7=14	3x7=21	4x7=28	5x7=35	6x7=42	7x7=49	8x7=56	9x7=63	10x7=70
8	0x8=0	1x8=8	2x8=16	3x8=24	4x8=32	5x8=40	6x8=48	7x8=56	8x8=64	9x8=72	10x8=80
9	0x9=0	1x9=9	2x9=18	3x9=27	4x9=36	5x9=45	6x9=54	7x9=63	8x9=72	9x9=81	10x9=90
10	0x10=0	1x10=10	2x10=20	3x10=30	4x10=40	5x10=50	6x10=60	7x10=70	8x10=80	9x10=90	10x10=100

0 x Anything = 0	1 x Anything = Anything	2 x Anything = Double Anything	5 x EVEN = Ends in 0 / 5 x ODD = Ends in 5	If One or Both Numbers are EVEN = EVEN / If Both Numbers are ODD = ODD	9 x Anything = 10 x Anything Less Anything	10 x Anything = Anything + 0

This Organizer was designed by Doris Wells-Papanek © 2004

Bibliography   Anderson, R.C. Concretization inn Sentence learning," Journal of Educational Psychology, 66, p. 179-183 (1974)

Carraway, Kimberly. President/Learning Specialist. Caraway Center for Teaching and Learning. Nashville, TN. Kimberly@CarrawayCenter.com

Douville, P., Pugalee, D., Wallace, J, and Lock, C. "Investigating the Effectiveness of Mental imagery Strategies in a Constructivist Approach to Mathematics Instruction," UNC Charlotte.

Gambrell, L.B., and Bales, R.J. (1986). "Mental Imagery and the Comprehension-Monitoring Performance of Fourth and Fifth Grade Poor Readers," Reading Research Quarterly, 21, p. 454-464.

Gambrell, L.B., and Jawitz, P.B. (1936). "Mental Imagery, Text Illustrations, and Children's Story Comprehension and Recall," Reading Research Quarterly, 28, p. 264-276.

Gerlic, I., and Jausovec, N.(1999) Multimedia: Differences in Cognitive Processes Observed with EEG. Educational Technology Research and Development, 47(3), 5-14.

Given, Barbara K. "Teaching to the Brain's Natural Learning Systems". ASCD 2002.

Greenleaf, Robert K. "Brain Based Teaching: Building Excitement for Learning." Published 1995. Updated 2000, 2005. Greenleaf Learning, P.O. Box 186, Newfield, ME 04056 www.greenleaflearning.com

Greenleaf, Robert K. "Creating and Changing Mindsets: Movies of the Mind." Updated 2000, 2005. Greenleaf Learning, P.O. Box 186, Newfield, ME 04056 www.greenleaflearning.com

Greenleaf, Robert K. " It's Never Too Late: " NASSP, www.greenleaflearning.com.

Greenleaf, Robert K. " Motion and Emotion: " NASSP, www.greenleaflearning.com.

Hannaford, Carla. "Smart Moves: Why Learning is Not All in Your Head". Great River Books 1995.

Hyerle, David. "Visual Tools for Constructing Knowledge," ASCD 1996.

Kovalik, S.J. and Olsen, K.D. "Exceeding Expectations: A User's Guide to Implementing Brain Research in the Classroom." www.books4educ.com, 2002.

Marzano, Pickering and Pollock. "Classroom Instruction That Works," ASCD, 2001.

Marzano, Robert. "Building Background Knowledge for Academic Achievement." ASCD, 2004.

Norton, John. Educator and Practicing Artist. Buckingham, Browne, and Nichols School, Cambridge, MA. john_norton@bbns.org

Pavio, A. (1983) "The empirical case for dual coding." as cited in: Imagery, memory, and cognition: essays in honor of Allan Paivio (J. C. Yuille, ed.) Lawrence Erlbaum Associates, Hillsdale, NJ.

Paull, Laura. Sixth Grade Language Arts Teacher. Lake Forest School District 67, Deerpath Middle School, Lake Forest, IL 60045.

Sadoski, Mark. "Mental Imagery in Reading: A Sampler of Some Significant Studies."

Sadoski, Mark. (1985) "The Natural Use of Imagery I Story Comprehension and Recall: Replication and Extension." Reading Research Quarterly, 20, p. 658-667.

Sadoski, M., Goetz, E.T., and Kangiser, S. (1988) "Imagination and Story Response: Relationship Between Imagery, Affect, and Structural Importance." Reading Research Quarterly, 23, p. 320-336.

Sadoski, M., Goetz, E.T., Olivarez, A., Jr., Lee, S. and Roberts, N.M. (1990) "Imagination in Story Reading: The Role of Imagery, Verbal Recall, Story Analysis, and Processing Levels." Journal of Reading Behavior, 22, 55-70.

Schenck, Jeb. Learning, Teaching and theBrain. knowa@wyodino.org, 2003.

Simkins, M., Cole, K., Tavalin, F., and Means, B. "Increasing Student Learning Through Multimedia Projects." ASCD 2002.

Smith, Karen A., Gouze, Karen R., "The Sensory-Sensitive Child: Practical Solutions for Out-of-Bounds Behavior." Harper Resource 2004.

Wells-Papanek, Doris. Tailored Tools and Learning Coach. Lake Forest, IL. doris@greenleaflearning.com

Zemke, Ron. Training/HRD. Jan 1981.

About the Authors

Dr. Robert K. Greenleaf

Dr. Robert K. Greenleaf has served as a professional development specialist at Brown University. With experience in all grade levels K-16, he has 20 of years of service in public education ranging from Superintendent of Schools to Assistant Superintendent of Schools, District Coordinator of Student Aspirations, Elementary School Principal, Teacher, and Special Education Assistant. He has also taught at the College level.

President of Greenleaf Learning, founded in 1987, Bob specializes in educational strategies for understanding behaviors, building esteem and achievement, and brain-based learning for long-term memory and recall. Bob is the author of seven instructional books, as well as many articles. He is the recipient of the "Outstanding Educator Award" from the Waterville Public Schools in Maine. Bob holds a Doctorate in Education from Vanderbilt University, a Masters in Educational Administration, and a Bachelor's degree in Psychology.

A past member of the National Speakers Association and Toastmasters International, he won several area and district speech events in the 1980's. His primary work is in the translation of research into practical applications for educators.

Contact Information: www.greenleaflearning.com

Doris Wells-Papanek

Doris Wells-Papanek is a design consultant and learning coach. She applies brain-based research to design tailored learning tools for education and business. In education, she consults with and coaches students, teachers, faculty, administrators, and parents to empower learners to organize their time, tasks, and thoughts. In business, Doris works with designers, industry, and design schools to integrate users' mindsets and learning processes into sustainable product development.

As a partner of Greenleaf & Papanek Publications, Doris is the co-author of five brain-based instructional books. With over 25 years of experience in design, software, and education, Doris has developed corporate design strategies, managed user interface groups, taught design, researched and designed human-centered usability studies, and designed the appearance and behavior of software. She has worked with companies such as Xerox, Apple, Lotus, Hewlett-Packard, Siemens, Philips, and Intuit. Her work has led to over 20 design and utility patents.

Doris holds a Bachelors of Fine Arts in Product and Environmental Design from the Kansas City Art Institute and School of Design.

Contact Information:
www.tailoredlearningtools.com

BOOKS FOR SALE *Greenleaf & Papanek* **Publications**

COLLEGE EDITION
Stock ID: **ETS-C** Price: **$27**

GRADES 5-12 EDITION
Stock ID: **ETS-S** Price: **$27**

ENGAGING TODAY'S STUDENTS, What All Educators Need to Know & Be Able to Do

In these two editions of "Engaging Today's Students," we have examined the research around the learner of today, effective teaching practices, and the brain sciences that link to long-term memory and recall. We have observed hundreds of classroom lessons and activities, developed by an array of practicing educators. A strong indicator for how we organized this book was our deep commitment to learners ~ students as learners AND teachers as learners ~ and how we all can learn in significant and sustainable ways.

With a central focus on what today's learners require, we have created two editions, one with a focus on College level learners and the other referencing the needs of the grades 5-12 population of students. Each addresses the four essential learning components that drive student engagement.

Memory, Recall, the Brain & Learning

Explore ways of incorporating brain-based instruction in the classroom. The power of combining verbal and visual representations into powerful bi-modal memory packets. Over 40 teacher and student generated activities, organizers, templates, and strategies. Improve student performance!

Stock ID: **MRBL** Price: **$25**

Brain Based Teaching

Explore teaching and learning through three overarching lenses: How can I "frame" (design) the learning circumstance or activity to INVITE ALL learners, to participate? How can I design the learning experience to CAUSE learner processing ~ the work required for sustained learning and recall? How do I engineer tasks that create opportunities for multiple PATHWAYS (connections) to be formed for integration, application, & recall?

Stock ID: **BBT** Price: **$24**

Coaching Reluctant Learners

This book provides today's middle and high school teachers with the tools they need to ensure classroom success for today's students in a practical framework ~ unit-by-unit, where both teacher and student can feel more successful. Embedded in this book are proven strategies, activities, examples, and a framework for units that will improve student motivation and performance.

Stock ID: **CRL** Price: **$27**

A Mastery Toolkit

Speaking directly to the student, this book explores the foundations of understanding, essential strategies, and learning tools to become motivated, independently engaged in the learning process, responsible for learning, and accountable for making good choices. The goal is to become a "Can Do" Student ~ a student who takes charge of their learning and empowers themselves in ways to be successful.

Stock ID: **AMT** Price: **$25**

Creating & Changing Mindsets

If rational behavior was the basis for human interaction and the mysteries of learning and development were well understood ~ this book wouldn't be needed. Clear strategies to assist "shifts" in attitude and behavior are included. The question, "will this change last?" plagues us every year. Here's how to impact changes within a month's time... for long-term, sustained differences!

Stock ID: **CCM** Price: **$24**

Greenleaf & Papanek **Publications**
PO Box 186 Newfield, Maine 04056

BOOK ORDER FORM

Please mail this form, to the above address, with a check, or

Fax a Purchase Order to:
fax   847.615.9958

bob@greenleaflearning.com
tel   207.793.8675

doris@tailoredlearningtools.com
tel   847.615.9957

NAME	
CO/ORG/SCHOOL	
ADDRESS	
CITY	
STATE/ZIP CODE	
EMAIL	
TELEPHONE	
CHECK or PO #	
DATE	

Make checks payable to **GREENLEAF LEARNING**.

For more information, please visit our websites:
www.greenleaflearning.com
www.tailoredlearningtools.com

For Discounts on Bulk Orders Over 10 Books Total: Call 207.793.8675

INSTRUCTIONS	DISCOUNT CALCULATOR

1 Enter the "Quantity" of each book you are buying

2 Add the total number of books and multiply by the "discount" amount using the "Discount Calculator"

3 Multiply "Quantity" x "Price" and enter the amounts due for each book in the "Totals" column

4 Add the extended total in the "Subtotal" box

5 Subtract the quantity discount and then add shipping fees to arrive to your final "TOTAL COST."

2 books total	=	**$1** discount per book
3 books total	=	**$2** discount per book
4 books total	=	**$3** discount per book
5-10 books total	=	**$4** discount per book

STOCK ID	QUANTITY	PRICE	TOTALS
ETS-C college		x $27	=
ETS-S grades 5-12		x $27	=
MRBL		x $25	=
BBT		x $24	=
CRL		x $27	=
AMT		x $25	=
CCM		x $24	=
discount	x =	subtotal	=
		less discount	-
		total	=
		shipping 1-4 books	+ $3.50
	additional shipping for more than 4 books add .50 cents each		+
		Canada add $3.00	+
		TOTAL COST	=